Mulk Raj Anand

A Man of Social & Humanistic Approach

Mulk Raj Anand

A Man of Social & Humanistic Approach

Dr. Rakesh Kumar Pandey

Raj Publications

New Delhi - 110002

Mulk Raj Anand: A Man of Social & Humanistic Approach

First Published in 2016

₹ 795

ISBN 978-93-82281-52-8

Published by : **Raj Publications**
108, 4855/24, Ansari Road,
Daryaganj, New Delhi-110002
Tel. : 011-23250939, 09811010939
E-Mail: rajpublications@yahoo.co.in
Website: www.onlinerajpublications.com

Laser Typesetting : Aarati Computers, Delhi-110 009

Printed at : Balaji Offset, Delhi

Dedicated to

My Parents

Late (Smt.) Gayatri Pandey

&

Late (Shri) Dhruv Pandey

Contents

Preface

Mulk Raj Anand was born in 1905 in Peshawar in present-day Pakistan. A pioneer of Indian writing in English, he gained an international following early in his life. His novels *Coolie* and *Untouchable* set an entire generation of educated Indians thinking about India's social evils that were perpetuated in the name of religion and tradition. These and other early novels and short stories brought into sharp focus the dehumanizing contradictions within colonized Indian society. Through his writings, he revealed that in addition to the foreign colonialism of Britain there existed layers of colonialism within Indian society. This internal colonialism stood in the way of India's transition to a modern civil society. While exposing the overarching divide between the British and a colonized India, he reveals an Indian society creating its own layers of colonizers and colonized thereby rendering the fledgling Indian nationalism an extremely problematic concept. Mulk Raj Anand was a founding member of Progressive Writers Association, a national level organization that wielded considerable influence during India's freedom struggle and beyond. An incredibly prolific writer, Mulk Raj Anand's creative career spanning a period of more than seventy-five years has been inextricably intertwined with the search for a just, equitable, and forward-looking India. He has written extensively in areas as variegated and diverse as art and sculpture, politics, Indian literature and history of ideas. He kept in constant touch with literary giants from across the globe, among them E.M. Forster who wrote a foreword to his novel, *Untouchable*. Mulk Raj Anand received the International Peace Prize from World Peace Council. Sahitya Akademi Award, "Padma Bhushan" and Leverhulme Fellowship are some of the awards and accolades during his long literary career. The Library of Congress has more than one hundred and fifty publications by and on him in its collection.

Along with R. K. Narayan and Raja Rao, Anand is credited with establishing the basic forms and themes of modern Indian literature written in English. At the core of his writing is a humanist philosophy that incorporates elements of socialist political and economic theory. Critics argue that his socially conscious works have shed keen insights on Indian affairs and enriched his country's literary heritage.

Mulk Raj Anand presents a real picture of Indian life in his novels. There is sincerity and immediacy in his realistic approach to his problems. If the themes here betray a sense of protest, it is a part of realism because realism is by no means a transcript of life only. Anand's social realism is sustained by his faith that an artist can contribute immensely towards social change. He is committed writer and his commitment, infact, was to liberate mankind and redeem the world from misery and pain by revealing the true nature of man with his inherent weaknesses. His purpose behind choosing underdogs as his protagonists was to awaken the conscience of the readers would over to work for the eradication of social injustice and exploitation from the society. His artistic vision includes all: Indian culture, customs, rituals, ethics and myths. His linguistic experimentations are undeniably carried out for the purpose of art as well as for the expression of fictional reality.

I am thankful to my family members and friends for their advice and words of encouragement, which made this work viable.

Last but not the least, my special thanks also go to the Raj Publications, New Delhi who brought out this book with an attractive get-up within a very short period of time.

--- Rakesh Kumar Pandey

1

Introduction

Mulk Raj Anand was born on 12 December 1905, as the third son of Lal Chand Singh and Ishwar Kaur in the Naushera Cantonment, fifteen miles away from Peshawar, now in Pakistan. The strong influence of both father and mother molded his character, thinking and attitude to life and the problems of living. For Anand, writing and life are inseparable; he has drawn extensively from personal experiences and from the experiences of those men and women close to him. Although he has written in a great variety of forms, his major achievement can be found in his series of autobiographical novels, *Seven Summers* (1951), *Morning Face* (1968), *Confession of a Lover* (1976). The other major autobiographical works are *Apology for Heroism* (1946) and *Conversations in Bloomsbury* (1981). Decidedly the most voluminous writer of the 'Big Three' of Indian fiction in English, the other two being Raja Rao and R.K. Narayan, all of whom commenced (commenced) writing in the nineteen thirties, Mulk Raj Anand has to his credit a mass of prose writing, all infused by intense experiences or life's significance and essence.

Anand portrayed the trials and tribulations of the

downtrodden, dispossessed and the poor with compassion. He felt the pain of the poor people, who belonged to lower class and weaved the thread of his novels around them. He made the people of India realize that the lower class, downtrodden and poor people are also human beings; they also have the right to live. In the Indian society when one is worshipping the animals like cows and bulls, the poor people are living in pitiable condition. Showing the worst condition of poor, Anand criticized the upper class, aristocratic people who had no care for humanity.

Everything has a reason behind it in this world. Anand's love and the feeling of compassion also had some certain reasons that lay in his past and in his surroundings.

Mulk Raj Anand was the son of a coppersmith turned soldier, Lal Chand who was head clerk in 38th Dogra Regiment. He had moved with his father as his regiment was transferred from place to place. Thus he saw many sections of Indian life and European life, the life of officers and the men of the Army. His mother was a peasant woman through whom he was nourished on the songs, tales, myths, and epics of the village community. He had known and seen and felt the rural life of Punjab and the North-West frontier provinces of those days. He had seen villages, groaning under poverty; he had seen village life sucked dry by parasites and religious priests. He closely observed the pitiable condition of untouchables and downtrodden people living around cantonment area. Anand's heart cried when he saw the injustice with the poor. All these had cast a spell on his mind and he decided to write about those people who were continually being insulted and injured by the British officers, the seminars, the money lenders, and the businessmen. He decided to be the mouthpiece of the underdog.

Anand treated his characters, not patronizingly, but with the sympathy and gave them a status of the respectable human beings. The sweeper, the peasant, the plantation labourer, the city drudge, the sepoy, all emerge alive from his novels-anguished and hungry, yet human superstitious and self divided, vividly realized in spite of their thwarted purposing. Anand portrayed the poor peasant, labourers, coolies, untouchables and uneducated people, fighting the desperate and loosing the battle of survival, in all his works whether it is a short story or a novel.

Anand was so much focused on the poor people that he did not write more about the orthodox and superior people of high caste, class and status in the town and villages where he had grown up. Anand's heroes are the downtrodden sweepers, coolies, the unemployed coppersmiths, the debt-ridden farmers and poor simple soldiers. Poverty and sufferance are the badge of their class. In his novels latrines, dirt, cuss-pools, poverty, beggary, prostitution and disease everything is there, beautifully expressed. Anand led this caravan of less miserable, and tells the west the story of the true India-not the India of bejeweled Maharajas, polo-playing European officers and club and drinks, but the real India of the majority of Indians. His purpose was not to draw sentimental tears but to show his readers the true dignity that is hidden behind poverty and disease.

Anand was aware of the weaknesses, folly, dissipation and ignorance of his pet characters but he wanted to show that these characters are good human beings in spite of their defects.

Anand's feeling of sympathy for the downtrodden was so intense that he started his career as a novelist with the novel *Untouchable* which presents the miserable condition of an untouchable in the Indian society. Anand had no faith in social norms.

When he observed that even animals are better placed on the earth of India than untouchables, he felt sympathy for such people and he decided to be the mouth pie (mouthpiece) underdog and did pain-staking effort to realize the reluctant people that untouchables were also human beings and they must be allowed to live with dignity.

That's why in his very first novel *Untouchable* he portrayed the character of Bakha, the protagonist, with sympathy and attracted people's attention towards the problems of untouchables. With a remarkable skill, Anand entered into Bakha's soul and exposed Bakha's helplessness, frustration, anxiety and agony to the degree that he had become an embodiment of Bakha himself.

Through some of his novels Anand brought forth the problems of upper class people who are poor and suffer because of lack of money. In *Coolie* Anand sympathetically portrayed the character of Munoo who in spite of being an upper class, strives for a place in society because he is not well off. In this novel, Anand threw light on the problem of child labour also. The novel becomes more touchy at the end when Munno dies of Tuberculosis. Through this novel Anand mourned not only for Munno but also for thousands of Munoos who died untimely because of being the victims of this materialistic society. Through elephant trainer, Anand presented the reality of the big cities where people are so materialistic that they had no care for humanity. Anand has vividly described the life of the laborers in a cotton mill, their exploitation, their overcrowded dwellings and their unhygienic toilets. The description is quite realistic and Anand's portrayal of the deplorable condition of poor laborers present Anand's humane approach for mankind.

Anand believed that poverty was amongst the main cause of human beings sufferings. It affects not only a person's life but also the life of his whole family.

In *Two leaves and a Bud,* Anand depicted the widening gap between the haves and the have not, the exploiters and the exploited, the rulers and the ruled. In this novel, Anand presented the story of an exploited peasant, Gangu who is killed while trying to protect his daughter from being raped by a British colonial official and his wife dies of a disease. Through Gangu, Anand portrayed the mental state of the laborers of tea-plantation who feel jeopardized while working under the ruthless masters. They are destined to suffer because they are deprived of money. In *Two leaves and a Bud,* Gangu tried hard but could not get a loan for the cremation of his wife. Anand's portrayal of Gangu's miserable condition is quite realistic. He successfully drew sympathy of the readers for Gangu who was roaming in the whirlpool of his destiny.

Anand always applied his philosophical mind to current social, political, economic problems; etc. His auto-biographical writings are stamped with the distinguishing quality found in his fictional work. More important for our study of Anand is that in the wide canvas of the auto-biographical novels, and in his other novels, characters, incidents and dialogues figure which are very closely based on characters, incidents and even dialogues from Anand's own life.

Mulk Raj Anand has his roots in the Punjab, the land or the five rivers, although he spent twenty years in England, 1925-1945. It would be no exaggeration if one sees that he has the distinction of being the only Indian writing in English whose themes are Indian. His characters speak mostly as Indians do, especially Indians of the Punjab, and whose novels have a style and form that are characteristically Indian. This becomes easy to understand because Anand responded to the heartbeats of the ancient tales and stories of Hindu epics and sagas of the Punjabis, Persians and Muslims – a mixture of mystery, music and local tradition, told to him by his mother in those first seven years of conscieusness (consciousness) encompassed in Seven

Summers. There was also a maternal uncle, viz. Mama Dayal Singh, a rustic young mystic, whose discourses on love and compassion influenced Anand in his search for truth and an ideology to answer his perplexities and perpetual quest in search of the meaning of life.

Anand speaks vehemently against the pro-British, half-baked education he received in the schools of the cantonment towns of Nowshera and Jhelum, at Amritsar and Ludhiana, and later in Khalsa College, Amritsar, 1921 -1925.

His strong nationalist attitude was inculcated in Anand as a young lad of seven by his mother and his maternal grandfather's family, who never ceased to oppose the British rulers because their farming lands had been confiscated and handed over to Harbans Singh, a sycophant of the administrators.

However, it was Anand's mentor-philosopher-tutor, Uncle Dev Chand, a failed M.A. of Amritsar, who introduced Anand to the atrocities of the political regime of the British Government in India, to the hardships of the society, to economic poverty and the crippling of Indian trades. Anand, the adolescent in school, came in the course of the next few years into contact with the Gandhian movement for India's freedom from imperialistic rule; all these felt-experiences are told extremely well in Morning Face.

The urge to write came to Anand from being a protester, the outcome of calf love for Yasmin, and the sister-in-law of his college's friend Noor Muhammad of Khalsa College. Anand had read a lot of poems by Dr. Iqbal, in particular.

The Secret of "Self", often quoted in *Confession of a Lover*, in the novels and journalist writings. Anand as a novelist projects a conception of himself and a conception of life which shows how much he was influenced by the intellectuals and others, mainly western European. They influenced him whether by philosophical systems, political ideologies or literary styles.

This period of his life came about when Anand left his home village in the Fall of 1925 on obtaining a B.A. (Hons) degree to pursue further studies in Philosophy at University College, London under the Gandhian Scholar Professor G. Dawos Hicks. He was to live in England 1945, making many friends among the famous Bloomsbury Group in particular, and other eminent English men of letters.

In England, Anand found he could not develop any roots because many great thinkers of the West were foretelling the doom of Western civilization.

The materialistic acceptance of life, current among the people, had no firm tenets that he could accept. It was at this state that Anand had been welcomed by the Leftists of Britain of the 1930's, for he readily subscribed to the idea of a brotherhood of writers with a role to play in the liberation, of people from political tyranny. He also joined the International Brigade for Peace and slipped into Spain in 1939. Though he did not get to the War Front for he admits he cannot bear to see blood spilt.

Although he came into contact with Marxism in 1926 and attended a Study Circle at the residence of Allen Hunt, the Trade Unionist, quite regularly, it was only in 1932 that he felt the full impact of Marx's philosophy. He accidentally came across Marx's *Letters on India* in the New York Tribune Herald issue of 1853 and on reading these Anand resolved to fight for the freedom of his country from imperialist rule and from a society whose class barriers, philosophy and orthodoxy combined to trap and stifle an impressive will, aspirations, intelligence, Anand and sensibility. Though his dominating creative in dooms himself poetic realism, later developed an advocate of humanism, social realism, into a philosophy of Karuna Rasa or compassion for the downtrodden and oppressed of society. In a letter to Saros Cowasjee, Anand wrote,

> The truth is that I had given up philosophical systems of all kinds to concentrate on writing from the heart - the wisdom of the heart if I may call it such, it was mere folly than wisdom. But, my sympathies with the, 30's movement, my gains from Marx and my feeling of repugnance against alien rule, did certainly incline me to sympathy with the Russian Revolution, even as I had inclined earlier to the ideals of the French Revolution, via Rimbaud. And, of course, there was the Indian struggle. How much of all this get into the novels I don't know. Anyhow, I am not in the least apologetic about the Karuna Rasa. I did not know this word completely until 1934 when I had written about five novels.
>
> I do not wish to deny the accusation of sympathy. Only a novel makes the sympathy flow and does not change people into leftists by falling on someone's head from a Shelf. I am not God. But I would say that I have tried to be sincere in facing up to people and am trying to create higher consciousness and intensity by splattering the blood all over, as the Elizabethans did on the stage.

Over the years Anand entered into similar correspondence with scholar critics and research students, explaining and defending himself and his creative art, and also defining his reactions to criticism and to political and intellectual challenges. In a conversation on 30 October 1979 in Bombay, Anand avers that his radical humanism is,

> ...the natural outcome of my searching's and sufferings; I had seen how the bureaucrats behaved during the General Strike of 1926 in England. My

> fight is aginst (against) the bourgeoisie, their small-mindedness and petty beliefs that affect all social relations.

Anand's work is a synthesis of many conflicting elements. His overriding concern is to preserve the best values of traditional India in contemporary society and to discard those which are redundant.

Anand has written down his confession of over 2000 pages in his long-hand scrawl, mainly out of love for his Irish girl friend Irene Rhys whom he met in 1926 while walking on Snowdon, in North Wales. No publisher accepted it in the I930e (1930). At Irene'e suggestion, Anand began to write novels and short stories about the people and personalities that had somehow and somewhere touched him in his Indian childhood and youth in the Punjab and elsewhere.

This is how the first draft of *Untouchable,* Anand's first novel came to be written. It was after Anand had read Gandhi's article on Uka, a sweeper boy living in the Sabarmati Ashram, published in Young India, that he sailed to India in 1932 for discussions with Gandhi in an attempt to understand his 'Harijan' philosophy. This meeting was to have a strong impact on Anand, as he himself has admitted in his writings. In *Untouchable,* Anand shows that though Bakha was impressed by Gandhi's talk, his exhortation to him to improve one's own life as a solution was not acceptable to Bakha, because it did not answer his real problem, namely, of finding an identity in a caste-ridden society. In *The Sword and the Sickle* Lalu the hero holds Gandhi up to ridicule because of his appearance and talk of self-purification and sarvodaya; Lalu wanted Gandhi to provide a solution to the dying and starving farmers. Gandhi's economic thought was to Anand's rational mind an impossible dream - the regeneration of the traditional village administration.

Having come under the full influence of Marxism, Anand favored mechanization and industrialization as remedies to alleviate poverty and the exploitation by moneylenders and landlords of the villagers. *The Big Heart* is a portrayal of the use of the machine and its effect on the coppersmith community of Kucha Ballarama Lane, in Amritsar.

Anand was well qualified to interpret the social and political concerns prevalent in pre-Independence India and to interpret the tidal movements that marked these eventful years before the imperialist rule was thrown off and Indians became masters of their own destiny as a nation.

Anand's novels also portray his experiments in love and soul-search.

He avers that he has kept on writing because there is a compulsion within him to put on paper answers to his quest for some philosophies or tenets that are acceptable to him as the only way to live with his fellow men. There is also the compulsion to express his feelings, his inner convictions and beliefs that have made him accept life during the many crises he has gone through. Behind his humanistic philosophy, now termed Karuna Rasa, he can bear his sufferings and the many crises of his life as a man of letters.

His first novel, *Untouchable,* was one of the many novels and short stories that have come from the 'Confessional', which never passed the state of a publisher's acceptance. As a novel, *Untouchable* is a microcosm of Anand's concerns and philosophy of life. It has been a success story from its publication in 1935, going into three editions in two months. Its publisher gave the struggling Anand an advance of 100 to write further, without considering whether the sales from the first edition would cover this amount.

To Anand, writing is not a profession; he asserts he does not write to earn a living and, in fact, does not make money out of writing. He once told Saros Cowasjee, in one of his letters addressed to this critic, about the problems he faced with foreign exchange on royalties, which are mainly from the translations of his works in many European languages, in particular, in East European countries. He is a writer with a prolific literary output in many literary genres. In his novels he experiments with theme, technique and style, on a scale never attempted by his equally well-known contemporaries, Raja Rao and R.K. Narayan. Recognition has come his way in abundance. The Government of India awarded him the Padma Bhushan in 1968. And India's Academy of Letters, The Sahitya Akademi, made its prestigious award to *The Morning Face* in 1971.

2

The Beginning of Writing

Anand is the most prolific Indian writer in English. His creative output spans a greater part of his life, from 1929 to the present. His greatest works are in fiction and short story. However, Anand has written much and, sometimes eloquently so, on a variety of subjects. As a rational Indian, he has found himself compelled to write on historical, cultural, political, educational, religious and philosophical aspects of Indian life and times. Besides, Anand is also famous as an art critic and his works on Indian art and architecture in particular are considered landmarks in themselves. There is also *Marg*, the outstanding art journal of India which Anand founded and edited, and which contains his best writings on art.

If a novel is turned down by as many as 19 publishers, who would not feel disappointed? This happened to Mulk Raj Anand before his well known novel, *Untouchable*, was published in 1935. At one stage, he felt so frustrated that he even thought of committing suicide. But the personal crisis was overcome in a somewhat unexpected manner.

One publisher agreed to publish the novel provided

E.M. Forster, the author of *A Passage to India*, wrote a Preface to it. This was done, and the novel was published. It proved to be such an immediate hit that Anand is remembered for it more than any other novel of his. Not only that, the publication of Anand's novel was a trail-blazer in what has come to be called Anglo-Anglian fiction. Soon after, at some interval of time, other gifted writers made their appearance.

These three writers are generally clubbed together in India. Perhaps another notable new figure who appeared on the scene during the next few years was Ahmed Ali. He published a novel with the title, *Twilight in Delhi*, which dealt with the declining years of the Mughal rule. But, this was during the turbulent phase of the partition of India. Soon after its publication, the author migrated to Pakistan with the result that it became the ancestor of a new stream of English writing which was based on Pakistan and not on India.

In a book dealing with one author, a reference to his contemporaries can be made but no more. One thing, however, needs to be said. Each one of them was different in his own unique way. R.K. Narayan, for example, is best known for his comic style of writing. Raja Rao has a philosophical bent of mind. This became more and more pronounced with the passage of time.

As a novel, therefore, his novel *Kanthapura* stands out in more than one respect.

A good deal has been written about each one of them. What marks out Anand is his socisal conscience. This is what linked him to Gandhiji's thinking. It was not an accident that after he had written out the first draft of his novel, he got in touch with Gandhiji.

Why did Anand encounter such a prolonged degree of resistance to the publication of his first novel? During the preceding century or so, a number of competent British writers had written novels about India. What they wrote was based on either history or romance. One or two Indians had also attempted something. The pioneer in this regard was the Bengali novelist Bankim Chandra Chatterjee, who had started writing in the last quarter of the nineteenth century. After one novel in English, he switched over to Bengali, his mother tongue, and stopped writing in English. In brief, no Indian writers of note had written fiction in English about India till then.

Anand was almost the first person to do so.

How he started doing it also needs to be described. Born at the beginning of the twentieth century, he spent his early childhood in British cantonments in north India. His father was working in the Indian Army as a middle level administrator and got transferred from place to place. His own birth took place in Peshawar cantonment in 1905. Anand wrote an autobiographical novel about his growing up years and called it *Seven Summers*. It is highly perceptive and is rich in those picturesque details which influenced his thinking during his childhood.

There is always a distinction between an autobiography and an autobiographical novel. Anand had planned to write an autobiography at one time but never got around to writing one. As to autobiographical novels, he published four of them. He published a portion of the fifth novel also but it remained incomplete. Going by *Seven Summers*, a couple of things stand out. One, that he was a curious child. He wanted an answer to whatever puzzled him. More competent in his knowledge of English than most other children of his age, he followed everything that the British did with great eagerness and a sense of curiosity. So much so that he started copying them in a variety of ways. This habit of his became so notable that he was even nicknamed as Pilpili Sahib. He also wrote a book with that name and it overlaps *Seven Summers* to quite an extent. This colloquial term in Punjabi was satirical in intent and implied that he copied the British in almost everything that he did or encountered.

How he took to reading also needs to be referred to.

At least on two occasions in his childhood, he was confined to bed for long stretches of time.

This encouraged him to take to reading as a habit. And since he admired the British and he was almost the best student in this subject in his class, it was but logical that his range of reading was much more than most of his contemporaries.

The pro-British aspect of his personality remained unchanged till his college days. It was during those years that the Jallianwala Bagh incident took place in Amritsar to which place he belonged and where he was enrolled in a school at that time. Both these factors made the whole experience much more disturbing than might have happened otherwise.

At one stroke, from being an admirer of the British, he turned anti-British.

He took part in some of the protests that were being organised in the city and had to spend one month in jail as well. As is generally believed, the Jallianwala Bagh incident was a turning point in Indian national history and it had a direct impact upon his thinking.

Despite some reservations that Indians had in supporting the British in their fight with Germany, the Indian attitude, on the whole, was helpful rather than otherwise. The British held out high hopes of rewarding those Indians who helped them in the war effort but a certain kind of disillusionment set in when the British failed to keep their word. Worse than that, they shot down approximately 400 people in a public garden which had only one entry and exit.

About 2,000 people had assembled when General Dyer issued the order to the crowd to disperse, otherwise they would be forcibly dispersed. There was hardly any time to think about what to do and, before long, General Dyer issued the order to shoot. Many more could have been killed except for the fact that the Gurkha regiment which he commanded had exhausted its ammunition.

This entire incident created such a hostile reaction against the British that when an anti-British movement started and Gandhi emerged as its leader, it did not take long for Anand to adopt a strong anti-British attitude. As a matter of fact, after 1919, Anand became an ardent supporter of the Indian National Congress and also of Gandhiji who had more or less established himself as its new leader.

A couple of years later, Anand finished his college at Amritsar and started looking for an opening. One lucky coincidence was that during those days when he was an undergraduate, Annie Besant happened to visit the college.

He interacted with her at some length. One of the things that emerged as an outcome of that interaction was that she advised Anand to go to England for further study. Besant could see that he was a bright and eager young man who, if he remained in India, would get drawn into the national struggle and land up in jail before long.

All this happened in 1923-24, about the time he finished his college education. There is no authentic record of what he did during those unsettled years. He did some odd jobs here and there. One of the things that he did was to go to Shimla where he became a private tutor to several of the hill princes. Himachal Pradesh did not exist at that time as we know it today. In that area, however, there existed a number of small states which were ruled by local chieftains. Anand somehow came in contact with a couple of them.

This experience stood him in good stead. Later, he utilised this experience to write a novel about an Indian prince.

Apart from his connection with Shimla, he frequently visited Lahore. One of the people he got to know there was Mohammed Iqbal, the leading Urdu poet. He became fairly close to him and one of the outcomes of that interaction was that it confirmed him in his plan to go abroad for higher education.

What triggered the act of his departure from India was the situation at home. By the time he passed out, Anand had become explicitly anti-British whereas his father continued to be pro-British. This led to a confrontation between the two. It also led to a scene between the two parents. Like any mother, she was partial to her son, Mulk Raj. The father recognised his talent but was uneasy about his independent thinking and rebellious ways.

The fact of the matter was that while the father showed considerable interest in his future, he was, however, more concerned about his own future. He was afraid that his son would sooner or later get arrested or something of that kind. This, in turn, would prejudice his standing with his British bosses to whom he was loyal in every way. The confrontation between them became so violent that on one occasion the father hit his wife while she was defending her son.

Rebellious as he already was, Anand there and then made up his mind to go abroad. Among those who helped to fund his foreign trip were Iqbal, the poet. Another was the then Principal of Khalsa College, Amritsar, from where he had passed out. Obviously, the Principal must have been impressed by the potential talent of this young man and gave him a loan out of his own pocket. The most crucial help came from his mother. She pawned some of her gold with a professional money lender and gave him whatever she could raise. Coming from a lower middle class family, this was a daring step to take but she took it.

In London, Anand got admitted to a course in Philosophy in the University College. Iqbal had also specialised in Philosophy, even though he was known as a poet before he went to Germany for his higher education.

Anand too opted to study Western Philosophy in London. Whether he was influenced by the example of Iqbal or not cannot be said for certain.

No record of the difficulties he faced in London in those early years is available anywhere. Perhaps the most notable thing that happened was that the professor under whom he studied was very helpful and secured him some kind of a scholarship. More than that, a few months into his course, he asked him to go out of London and spend some quiet time in Wales. Till then, he had hardly any background in Philosophy. His teacher wanted him to read the classics and bring himself equal to the same range of reading and level of understanding as his other contemporaries had. Armed with a packet of books, he settled down somewhere in Wales and started studying.

During his stay in Wales, he came across an Irish girl, Irene, who played an important part in his life. He was captivated by her charm and personality and he did not hesitate to express his liking for her. As time went by, she became fond of him. Her father was also a university teacher and looked upon him as a bright young man in whom his daughter was interested. In later years, this fact played an important role in his life.

Years later, he wrote a book which he published about the time when he was proposing to return home after some 20 years of stay in UK. This book was called *An Apology for Heroism: A Brief Autobiography of Ideas*. This book along with another book, entitled *Conversations in Bloomsbury*, published in 1981, gives a somewhat detailed picture of how he evolved as a young, thinking person. A study of both these books throws a good deal of light on his life during those hectic days. No more need be said about them at this stage.

What is relevant to note here is the fact that what he saw of British life in UK was markedly different from what he had seen in India. In India, the British were the imperial masters. In UK, the situation was different. He had been impressed by the dignity which even those who may be described as menial workers conducted themselves. This was unlike what he had lived through in India.

Not everything that he saw came across in glowing terms. For instance, he made a shocking discovery when the General Strike of 1926 took place. It was opposed, among others, by his fellow students in the University College. The British miners who constituted the backbone of the Labour Party led this strike. That the strike did not succeed was another thing. He was in favour of the strike but it was only a small group of students who had adopted this attitude. On the whole, however, his first impression about UK was favourable. One instance of it may be quoted here.

In England, he found no such thing as untouchability as he had encountered in India. He has recorded one instance in *Seven Summers* which had made a profound impact on his thinking. The hero of the novel *Untouchable* was a sweeper boy, Bakha. Anand was very friendly with him and admired him in a number of ways.

One incident that had happened when he was growing up may be recalled here. Once, Anand was injured while at play. The sweeper boy took care of him in every way and took him home. Anand's mother, instead of feeling grateful for the care extended to her son, rebuked the sweeper boy for having physically touched him and made him impure. Anand was baffled by what he saw. What the sweeper boy had done was a normal human thing—to help someone who had been injured—and he had no intention of doing anything which would undermine or outrage any one's belief in Hinduism. As a matter of fact, the sweeper boy was also a Hindu but an untouchable!

This was something which profoundly disturbed Anand and he found it difficult to accept. What he saw in England was qualitatively different.

There was no question of anyone being regarded as an untouchable. A human being was a human being and there was nothing else to it. This aspect of Hindu society in which he had grown up bothered him and upset him profoundly. What he saw in UK was a preview of life which he regarded as acceptable. What was happening in India was unacceptable to him and to the kind of society which he wanted to see established in India.

During his stay in Wales and the close interaction he had with Irene, he talked freely to her about his early childhood, his various experiences and so on. There developed such a close bond between them that, partly because he had found someone sympathetic in Irene, and partly driven by his own personal experience, he started writing a kind of confession for her. Irene encouraged him to do so and he reduced the story of his childhood to writing. While Anand wrote in long hand, Irene typed it out.

Regardless of whether that manuscript still exists or not, the fact remains that much of his later writing can be traced back to what happened in those early years of his life. When he took to novel writing in a professional way, he was writing on the basis of what he had gone through and recorded in that manuscript. The more important thing to understand is that Anand's youth coincided with the new political awakening that was taking place in India during those years. It was a period of social turmoil. Things that had been accepted for centuries together now came to be questioned. The Western ways of thinking began to make an impact on Indian society. The steady emergence of the movement for Indian freedom acquired a mass character under the influence of Gandhi. Before long, Anand got drawn into it.

Untouchability was one unacceptable dimension of what he saw and he began to question it. Many other things too were being questioned. Not only that, the imperialist hold on India was also being questioned. The link between imperial rule and the feudal setup that held India under siege was also under attack. There was estrangement between the Hindus and the Muslims, and as time went by, the British started to fish in trouble waters.

Being a sensitive and thoughtful young man, Anand reacted to all these things in a manner that, years later, when his writing career took on, his sociological imagination and vision could not but assume a prominent role in it.

To come back to the 1926 Strike, Anand had found it a somewhat disturbing experience. Before long, he came to the conclusion that the bulk of Englishmen and women stood for the kind of status quo which imperialism represented in the rest of the world. He had seen ample evidence of it in India and, now, for a change, he witnessed it even in UK.

The rise of the labour party, the new emerging political force, took another 3-4 decades to come to power. It was only in 1945 that the Labour Party won a decisive victory. It had won a victory of sorts in the early 30s as well but it was not decisive enough to change the political situation as it might have.

Anand's interaction with Irene proved to be exceptionally productive as far as his own personal growth was concerned. She not only typed out his manuscript, they both became so close to each other that, together, they visited the continent for several days and went around Paris and various other places. This was his first visit to the continent and he found it both educative and stimulating. The funding for this visit had come from Irene's father.

Irene was active in the Irish movement for independence. At one stage, she was arrested and put behind the bars. Anand visited her in jal! and remained in touch with her almost all the time. What is relevant here is the fact that Irene, being both a thinker and a doer, influenced Anand profoundly. His decision in 1945 to return to India after two decades in England was to quite an extent influenced by the example of Irene. There is more to be said on this subject which will be taken up later. We now move on to how *Untouchable,* his first novel, came to be written and in what circumstances it was published.

Untouchable and after of all things that Anand experienced in childhood, nothing distressed him more than the issue of people being regarded as untouchables. Students of history know that this was one of the foremost issues in the 20s of the last century. Gandhi led a systematic campaign against this evil social practice.

He visited several parts of India where this problem was more acute than elsewhere. Kerala was one of those states which he visited in the latter half of the 20s. In that State, even the shadow of someone who was regarded as 'impure' upon another person who was not 'impure' was strongly objected to.

Ever since he had become an adult, Anand had identified himself with the dispossessed and the underprivileged. As a part of this outlook on life, he looked upon Gandhi as an innovator in Hindu society. More precisely, his experience as a child persuaded him to write something on the subject. There was an incidental story in Gandhi's weekly newspaper, Harijan, about a young untouchable boy which excited Anand's imagination. Prompted by that, he wrote a letter to Gandhi asking for an appointment with him. Gandhi promptly replied in the positive. As hinted earlier, perhaps Anand was already busy writing something on the theme of the equality of all human beings.

At this stage, it is important to recall his experiences in London which are discussed in some detail in his book, *Conversations in Bloomsbury*. As is clear from a reading of this book, Anand had got drawn into what was generally known as the literary life of England soon after his initial stay in London. Leonard and Virginia Woolf, a well known literary couple, generally played host at the time to some of the leading writers of the day in their home in Bloomsbury It was located in the heart of the central London.

Being almost next to the British Museum and encircled by some of the better known bookshops in London, it was an ideal location for the weekly meeting of some of the leading writers of the time.

Leonard Woolf had worked in Ceylon, as it was known then, for a few years as a civil servant. But he soon chose to resign and returned to London.

He established a publishing house, called the Hogarth Press, and started publishing the writings of some of those people who mattered in the world of letters. Anand somehow got to know Leonard and started correcting proofs for him in order to supplement his income. This in turn put him in contact with a number of leading writers and made him sensitive to the currents and cross currents of contemporary literary life.

James Joyce was a leading writer of that period. Anand had read him extensively. One of the things that impressed him after a reading of his *Ulysses* was that he had compressed the happenings of the events in one of his novel into one day.

Following that model, Anand attempted a novel, entitled Bakha. Bakha, as referred to earlier, was a sweeper boy who had been a friend of his as a child. Anand decided to write about him and projected him as the hero of his novel. Eventually the title of the novel was changed to *Untouchable*.

It was during this period in his life that he came very close to Irene. He would write out something and she would type it out for him. How to go and see Gandhi who had responded so promptly? He had to find money to travel back to India and it was not so easy but somehow he managed it. He had gone to London in 1925 and his first journey back to India was in 1929. A couple of years later, be revisited India and this time he came back with the manuscript of his maiden novel which he read out to Gandhi and rewrote it substantially in the light of what Gandhi had told him.

At that time, Gandhi lived in Sabarmati Ashram, Ahmedabad. As arranged, he went to the Ashram. He was dressed like an Englishman at that time. The moment Gandhi saw him in his corduroy jacket; Gandhi expressed disapproval of his dress. Indeed, without asking for his consent, Gandhi told Mahadev Desai, his secretary, to give him some khadi clothes. After he had changed into the Indian dress, Gandhi had another meeting with him and asked him about his mission.

Anand told him about the novel that he had written. Gandhi's first observation was that he might write a pamphlet rather than a novel but, on Anand's insistence that he preferred a fictional mode of communication, Gandhi did not press his point any further. For the next several weeks, at an appointed hour of the day, Anand would read out one chapter of the novel at each sitting and Gandhi gave his reactions to what was read out. But before this could be done, Gandhi had told Anand that there were three conditions which he would have to fulfill.

The first one was that he would not drink. Anand replied honestly to the effect that while he had been drinking in London, he would not do so in the Ashram. The second condition was that he would not look upon any woman with a feeling of desire. To this, Anand replied that he would act as desired but he could not forget his girl friend in England who, among other things, had helped him come to India. Gandhi accepted this contention without any further discussion. Thirdly, he would have to clean the latrines like other members of the Ashram. Anand accepted this condition readily.

One important outcome of his long stay in the Ashram was that Gandhi told him in no uncertain terms and in convincing detail that his characters should not speak like Bloomsbury intellectuals. On the contrary, they should speak like ordinary men and women whom Anand had encountered in the course of his growing up. This was a piece of advice which made him reexamine his assumptions. To refuse to accept social discrimination as a fact of life was perfectly in order. But how to express it in terms of conversation in daily life was something that he had yet to learn. To some extent, Gandhi taught him that.

To cut a long story short, the novel got condensed by

about one third.

With that draft in his pocket, Anand revisited his family in Amritsar and travelled around the country for quite some months. Travelling around the country was one of the things suggested to him by Gandhi. He told him that he had gone to England for higher study but had had very little experience of life in India. If he wanted to be a writer, one of the things to do was to go around the country and understand it better. Anand acted upon this advice and visited different parts of India during the next few months. Among other places, he revisited Kangra where he had spent some time during his childhood. He also visited the Assam tea gardens. Sometime later, when he published his novel, *Two Leaves and a Bud,* he based it on his visit to Assam.

Let us come back to *Untouchable.* After his return to London, he got busy with a book on Persian Painting and another on The Hindu View of Art.

These two were specialised books and there was an established market for them. In another year or so, he was almost ready with his manuscript of *Untouchable* and started looking around for a publisher. But no one was prepared to publish it. It is important to understand why.

While a number of British citizens who had lived in India had written novels about India, their point of view was essentially imperialist in character. One important example of it was the kind of fiction that Rudyard Kipling had written. His novel, *Kim,* had proved immensely popular. If Kipling eventually went on to win the Nobel Prize for Literature, one important feature of his work was the imperial view of India which he had projected. This perception of India was generally accepted in the West.

Indeed, it was the prevalent view about India in the Western world, at least till then.

In the 1920s, E.M. Forster's novel, *A Passage to India,* was published.

There was something fresh about it. The point of view projected here was more humanistic than imperialistic. After *Kim,* this was one novel which had compelled attention, so to speak. Forster had spent quite some rime (time) in India and understood the country much better than the earlier generation of imperialist writers.

What Anand now attempted went much beyond E.M. Forster. Two things about him and his novel were unmistakable. One was his unconcealed hatred of imperialism.

This was at odds with the kind of writing that Kipling and most others had been doing. The other important dimension of his writing was his total disapproval of and disgust with the kind of feudal life which he had witnessed and lived through in India. His opposition to the; caste system and his fervent belief in the equality of all human beings dripped from every word that he wrote.

What was the motive power behind his writing? His own answer is revealing. In his book, *Apology for Heroism,* he states:

> I had come abroad, not merely with the purpose of sightseeing (sightseeing), but with the vague and genuine ambition to learn the secrets of European civilization, to reside for a time in a world where ideas of social and human equality could at least be discussed freely, if they were not quite sincerely accepted.

This very idea is expressed a little more graphically later in the same book:

> I struggled to weigh up the double burden on my shoulders, the Alps of the European tradition and

> the Himalayas of my Indian past, all my senses aching to realise the significance of the history of my country, all my heart and brain devoted to the search of those causes which had led to its present degeneracy.

These two quotations illustrate the kind of mental and emotional thinking with which he wrote *Untouchable.* Everything came from his heart. The hero of the novel, Bakha, has a number of hectic experiences which, following the model of James Joyce, he compressed into one day. Each experience is different in character but each one of them illustrates how he is treated as an untouchable all the time. As E.M. Forster who wrote the Preface to the novel pointed out, the novel has a form though not a tight structure. Even though some people think that it is loosely constructed, that is not exactly so.

Towards the end of the novel which, in a sense, reveals, and indeed underlines his marginalised existence as a sweeper boy, Bakha has three options open to him. One is to listen to the words of a missionary who wanted to convert him to Christianity. This might ease his situation to some extent but would not solve the problem. The second was to go by the wise and gratifying words of Gandhi who told his countrymen that to look upon anyone as an untouchable was not the right thing to do. Everyone was pure or impure in the same measure, and to look down upon anyone was not right. The third choice was that the new technology adopted in the West be adopted in India also so that human refuse is washed out, and no one can be labelled as a sweeper. The third option made good sense to him, and Anand leaves the matter at that.

It is not necessary to go into further details except to make the point that Anand was talking about a world which was so distant for the English speaking reader that they had only heard about the situation in India and not seen it in the disturbing manner in which Anand had described it. If the novel was not published, the principal reason was that Anand's point of view was not seen to be familiar with the English speaking reader. At least, that is what the publishers thought. It was the overwhelming popularity of the novel which made them reconsider their earlier conservative, indeed overcautious, perception of the taste of the reading public. The fact of the matter was that times were changing but the publishers had not yet understood the changing ethos of the age.

Once it was published, public support to it was immediate and overwhelming. It was eventually translated into around 40 languages of the world.

That kind of initial resistance and eventual resounding success is not an unknown phenomenon in literature. There are several examples where what is called consumer resistance comes in the way of a new kind of writing being published. Once it is published and wins public acclaim, the earlier barriers are overcome, and the kind of sensibility which new writers project comes to be accepted readily as well as enthusiastically. Anand's distinction lay in this fact that he was the first man to overcome this kind of consumer resistance and, in the process, projected his unique kind of sensibility.

As soon as *Untouchable* was published and once the critical doors were opened to him, Anand followed it up with his next novel. *Coolie,* which had been germinating in his mind for a long time. Indeed, it (delete) was written within three months of the publication of *Untouchable*. For Anand, this was some kind of a breakthrough. He had been struggling to express himself in his own distinctive way. Once the artificially manufactured kind of resistance which had delayed the publication of his first novel had been overcome, Anand started drawing upon his earlier experience of life and came out with many more novels and short stories.

The hero of *Coolie* is a 14 years old boy, nicknamed as Munnoo. He belonged to Kangra Valley, then a part of Punjab. Anand had known that part of Punjab right from his childhood and he revisited it on his first visit to India after his half decade's stay in UK. Over the years, this Valley had come to have the reputation of supplying a large number of domestic servants to the newly emerging middle class of Punjab.

Once Munnoo got to the plains, he became a domestic servant in the family of a junior officer in one of the banks. He does a series of jobs as a domestic servant, a worker in a pickle factory, then a textile factory and so on. Each job represents a different phase of his bitter experience. His last job is with an Anglo Indian lady in Shimla where he had to pull a rickshaw for her. Owing to the unsanitary conditions in which he had to live, he got infected by tuberculosis. This proves fatal and he succumbs to the disease in the end. Altogether, we see him functioning only for two years and each job is a story of his unrelieved misery and exploitation.

While *Untouchable* had confined itself to the experiences of one day in Bakha's life, Munoo has a different kind of career. He flies from one job to another and it turns out that each one of them is worse than the earlier one.

In both cases, it is an instance of exploitation by those controlling the social set up in which these two characters find themselves. Anand describes the successive stages of this desperate struggle for dignity with profound concern and compassion.

These two novels revealed a dimension of India's social

life which had not been unveiled earlier by anyone in Indo-Anglian fiction. A leading British critic, V.S. Pritchett, wrote in a letter to Anand, "I got more out of Coolie than any other novel I have read for a long time, indeed. It is the only political novel which has profoundly satisfied me." This comment was made in March 1937.

As an extension of his commitment to social causes, Anand got drawn into the anti-fascist movement which was then emerging in Europe. Not only that, he went on to participate in the Spanish Civil War which was raging at that time. Indeed, he spent three months in Spain. Anand was perhaps the only Indian writer to have done so. So many others belonging to different countries were involved in this adventure which had a pronounced antifascist bias.

No wonder when he came out to India in the following year, he was already a famous man. As the author of two widely acclaimed novels and as having participated in the Spanish Civil War, Anand came to have a reputation which signified that here was a man who had something new to say. Not only that, having taken a consciously anti-Imperialist stance and written about those aspects of Indian life which had hardly been touched upon earlier, there was something distinctive and unique about him.

The Nehru family was one among the other people he got to know in the course of his visit. Nehru's sister, Krishna, became a close friend and the two of them later collaborated in writing a book, titled *The Indian Bride*. Jawaharlal himself extended patronage to him. He spent some time in Allahabad and acted as Jawaharlal's political secretary for a few weeks. These things are being referred to here because they were destined to play a helpful role in his later career when he returned to India after 1945.

It may be added here that during his entire writing career, and even today, Anand is mainly known for these two novels. As far as one can judge, even in the decades to come, the kind of Indian reality which Anand projected would be historically difficult to ignore. For one thing, he was almost the first writer in English to project this issue. For another, that reality has not yet undergone a qualitative change.

Almost every feature of it—its extent, spread, coverage, character, the feudal hang ups that stem from it and, above all, the sheer fact of exploitation by those who shamelessly indulge in it—are so stubbornly present even today that Anand continues to be relevant, even contemporary, both socially and artistically. And this was no mean achievement.

After he had completed his doctorate from University College, London, he did not choose to return to India but attempted to establish himself as a professional writer there. He had some success in it in so far as he was able to publish two books on art criticism which have been referred to above.

Meanwhile, he had written the novel which was eventually called *Untouchable*. At one stage, he even toyed with the idea of writing a play rather than a novel.

That apart, having published two novels in the idiom that he had worked out for himself, he wanted to do more of that kind of writing. He theorised about it in the following manner:

It is only by extending the range of one's sympathies to all human beings and by concentrating on all that exalts them that we can rescue the disinherited from the morass of superstition and poverty in which they are steeped. But mercy and generosity and love for humane causes ought not to blind us to the evils, the falsities and stupidities that prevent goodwill from emerging among human beings. Nor should false notions of personality as a mere bundle of personal desires limit the conception of man as an improving animal.

At this point of time, Anand made a trip to India. In 1936, a new body called the Progressive Writers Association had got established. The main person behind this initiative was Sajjad Zaheer. Anand had known him from his London days. Indeed, they had become close friends. When this writers' body was set up and its first meeting was held in Lucknow under the chairmanship of Munshi Prem Chand, Zaheer became the Secretary of that organization. In short, the transition from being a writer to an activist did not require much effort on his part. It all looked so natural.

Restless as he always was, Anand moved about a good deal during those days and made a large number of fresh contacts. Some of the people he had known earlier during his stay in London had come back to India and were doing, a variety of jobs and following different professions. No wonder, Anand spent several months in going around the country and getting to recontact these people. As a matter of fact, the contacts made at that time were so numerous and so close that Anand paid yet another visit to India in 1938. It is equally important to remember that Anand did not neglect his writing. In 1937, he brought out a new novel with the title, *Two Leaves and a Bud*.

It excited considerable controversy, and to some extent, if the British tea owners felt upset about how they had been depicted, this should not have come as a surprise to him. Years later, looking back over the publication of this particular novel, he made a comment which may be reproduced here, "I conceived *Two Leaves and a Bud* as a poem of suffering. I admit that it is the most bitter of my novels, but it is poetic; were it a literary reportage, it would have been hundred times bitterer".

The reasons for giving these details are that these early

novels by Anand gave him a certain kind of moral and literary projection. The two basic elements in that projection were that Anand understood the life and longings of his people in India. He projected their struggles almost in the manner in which several of the writers writing in Indian languages were writing. They were in closer touch with things as they were happening, and truly speaking, there was hardly any distance between them and the common people. That is why they were so authentic. Munshi Prem Chand was a prime example of this kind of writing and there were many others in various other Indian languages.

Secondly, Anand was the first writer in English to write about this exploited segment of Indian society. In doing so, he had fought many a battle. Eventually he had his way and that is what explains the verve and the authenticity of the first phase of his writing career. It lasted from 1935 when his first novel was published to 1937 when his novel about the ruthless exploitation going on in the Assam tea gardens was published.

His overall perception is best described in the following lines which are taken from a letter he sent to one of his critics, "Man's fate, today, is no longer in the hands of the gods, but is often in conflict with the evil in other men. Man makes himself, or thinks he can".

The heart and mind of contemporary man is, therefore, moved by other casualties than salvation.

While something has been said about his writing career after the publication of his first-phase novels, no one had visualised that the Second World War would come so soon, and in a sense, Anand would get trapped in London. It is that phase of his career which requires to be discussed now.

3

The War Years

Anand's 1938 visit in India was spread over several months. Apart from everything else, he visited different parts of India. As stated earlier, this was in keeping with the advice given to him by Gandhi on one of his visits to India that he should see much more of the country than he had done till then.

There were two cities which attracted him more than others. One was Bombay. It was much more cosmopolitan than any other city in India and the other was Lahore.

He had known Lahore right from his childhood. Not only that, he had spent quite some time in that city. Culturally speaking, it was a lively city, and both during this visit and his subsequent visits after the end of the war, Lahore remained the centre of his activities to quite an extent. Iqbal, the famous Urdu poet, who was a kind of mentor for him, had also lived in Lahore. Since Anand was fairly close to him and the latter had also subsidised a part of his fare to London, it stands to reason that he must have spent some time with him also, though, when he returned for good to India in 1945, Iqbal had passed away by then.

One incident described by Khushwant Singh (he was personally present when it happened) about the 1938 visit to Lahore may be referred to here. It shows how the kind of neo-colonial thinking which had captured the thinking of most of the English speaking crowd in India refused to die down.

The colonial masters had come to terms with what Anand had stood for, but the neo-colonials found it more difficult to do so.

After the publication of his first three novels, he had a better grasp of the English speaking world. No other Indian had been able to overcome the barriers of ignorance or neglect which was the fate of most Indian writers writing in English then as he had done. Years later, in 1977 to be precise, when he recalled the intellectual struggle of those early days, he observed in an essay, titled *The Story of My Experiment with a White Lie,* I certainly felt in the midst of my poetry and exile, the compulsion that it is better to win applause by conforming to any establishment, but to face the privileged order, and to claim the right to notice the existence of a man like Bakha.

Before long, his early novels came to be compared to the early work of Dickens who, when the Industrial Revolution in the early nineteenth century was getting into stride, had unveiled certain dimensions of life which had not been brought to public light till then. Anand had not only given evidence of a firsthand knowledge of how the poor and the marginalised lived, he had also made two of them the heroes of his novels. *Two Leaves and a Bud,* his third novel, during those years, which had appeared before his 1938 visit to India, had also provoked considerable controversy. It had focused upon the exploitation of a poor family from Punjab which had been misled into seeking a better living in the Assam tea gardens.

The leading organization of tea planters in Assam was politically influential. Though Anand was able to effectively rebut their criticism of his work for being anti-British, particularly with the help of official documents (the Whitley Report on Assam tea gardens and the rest), the tea planters managed to have that particular novel banned in Assam. Such a step generally makes the book even more popular and this is precisely what happened in this case too. It may have got banned in Assam but elsewhere it was on sale. By that time, Anand had forged a place for himself in the literary landscape both of England and India. After 1947, when the novel was no longer banned, he re-published it with a fresh introduction.

One thing which he had done more or less extensively was that he thought in Punjabi and translated some of the colloquial and picturesque expressions into English, more particularly words of abuse and sacrilege, for the benefit of the non-Punjabi speaking readers. This was breaking new ground, and for years together, people continued to refer to this practice as an innovation.

But Anand himself has recorded somewhere that, to some extent, he had carried forward a practice which Kipling had started earlier. Only he made the whole thing a part of the artistic presentation of Punjabi life which he was seeking to project in a picturesque manner.

To come to the point, during his stay in Lahore, he was given a reception by some of the elite citizens of the city. They consisted mainly of lawyers, Indian members of the civil service and some senior officials. The idea was to honour him on his achievement as a writer. Some of the people present were not so enthusiastic about him. A couple of them went to the extent of saying that, given an opportunity, they too could have done the same thing.

Anand listened to all that in silence and with a sense

of dignity. Obviously they were reluctant to concede to him what people elsewhere had conceded readily as well as generously. When it became too much, he simply walked out. Before doing so, he told them that they had to produce an acceptable piece of writing, get it published and then talk in the manner they were talking. Those who wielded power in India under the patronage of the British were not prepared to go as far as the British critics had gone. This was not true of most places in India. Maybe there was also an ill-concealed sense of rivalry with some one (someone) who had chosen to stay on in UK and had eventually made his way and won public acclaim.

He travelled all over the country, and more notably, to Calcutta and Bombay. The anti-fascist sentiment was growing in the country. Anand was looked upon as some kind of a glamorous figure and he basked in the glory that his writing had earned him. As referred to earlier, the Nehrus took to him warmly, and when Anand returned to England in early 1939, he came back with the feeling that he had made his name as a gifted writer and now it was up to him to build upon that.

He had not worked out anything definite in his mind. The only thing that came as a surprise to him was that the war with Hitler came so soon. In the beginning of 1939, things were moving in the direction of a war but his guess was that it would take a little longer to break out than it actually did.

One unavoidable outcome of this development was that, whether he wanted it or not, or had so planned it or not, he had no choice but to spend the war years in London.

The British government, without consulting anyone in India, took the decision that India too was at war with Germany. After the 1937 election in India, the Indian National

Congress had captured power in more than half a dozen major provinces. The real power at the Centre was, however, wielded by the Viceroy. The federal part of the Government of India Act, 1935, under which things had to be reorganised differently, did not get enforced, largely owing to the reluctance of the Indian princes to give up their old ways of functioning. The British had not chosen to pressurise them in any way.

Since the Congress Party did not accept that India too was at war with Germany, there was a marked divergence of approach between the former and the Indian government. The next few years saw all kinds of developments, including the mobilization of the entire country in favour of the war effort, the rise of Jinnah as a political force, and the eventual partition of the country in 1947.

Without going into any of these details, what needs to be noted is that Anand found himself in an unenviable and difficult position. Living in England during those years was not easy. His own point of view was that he was anti-fascist in any case and was opposed to Hitler as much as anyone else was. The real problem was that India was being taken for granted by the British government as a participant in the war against Hitler and no attention whatsoever was being paid to India's servile status. The Congress Party wanted an arrangement to be worked out in terms of which, if this party cooperated with the British in the war effort, there would be a public assurance from Britain that, at the end of the war, India would be more or less free of the imperial hold.

In this connection, he brought out a book, called Letters on India, in 1942 which accused the British of exploiting India and not doing what ought to have been done at this stage of the war against Hitler. Broadly speaking, Anand's position was in conformity with that of the Indian

National Congress. It should not be necessary to go into details or trace the ups and downs of the Congress policy in its dealings with the British government.

While Atlee, the Labour leader, was a member of the British Cabinet, the important thing to remember is that the Prime Minister was Churchill. He had a blind eve (eye) as far as India was concerned. At one stage, Churchill went to the extent of saying it in so many words that he had not become the first minister of the King in order to liquidate the British Empire.

These details have been provided in order to underline the point that Anand was faced with a very difficult personal choice. On the one hand, he had brought out several novels which depicted the imperial exploitation of India and its unspoken support to the feudal forces which, in rum, were collaborating with the British government, and on the other hand, Anand was invited by his friend, George Orwell, to participate in the anti-German propaganda launched by the BBC. Orwell, a major figure in the British intellectual circles, was appointed director of this programme by the BBC.

He and Anand had been friends for a number of years. The two were so close to each other that a critic in USA has gone to the extent of writing a book, entitled *George Orwell and the Radical Eccentrics*. One of the four authors covered was Mulk Raj Anand. When Orwell wanted him to be a part of the BBC anti-Nazi campaign, Anand found it difficult to go with him beyond a point. There were unmistakable differences of political approach between them.

Anand was not an unknown figure in Britain at that time, if it may be added here. He had published a series of novels in about half a decade and his work had been widely appreciated. Stephen Spender looked upon him as an important revolutionary novelist. He remained busy with his literary work during these years. It was also during this period that he brought out what is called the Lalu trilogy. It was based on his perception of rural life in Punjab in the World War I era. On the whole, the first two novels of this trilogy were widely appreciated but the third one fell somewhat flat.

Obviously Anand had not been able to sustain the same level of competence and creativity in the third novel as he had attained in the earlier two novels. It seemed to lack the sureness of touch of the earlier two novels.

At any rate, as the war went on and Russia came under attack from Germany and the political climate began to change, the distance between Anand and people like Orwell began to diminish. Consequently, Anand started participating in the BBC programme. Perhaps it would be in order to quote Anand himself to explain his position more precisely:

> The one question that has been taxing my mind is how to reconcile that (Congress Party) affiliation with my belief that fascism would destroy all I stand for. I am afraid the British government had done nothing which may help to solve the dilemma which faced some of us. It had declared neither its war aims, nor its peace aims and India seems to be its one blind spot.

As stated above, Anand found it difficult to work out a mode of functioning which would be consistent with his position as a revolutionary thinker and radical writer. Over the years, he had worked out a certain way of working for himself. This was manifested in the novels that he had written. They marked him out as a man who stood for a certain set of culturally progressive political values. Basically, he was a humanist, if it may be added.

The circumstances of his life had placed him in a

situation where, had he been located in India at that time; he would have, perhaps, participated in political activities in line with the thinking of the Indian National Congress. Since he was obliged to be in England during those years, he conducted himself with dignity and a sense of commitment which he did not wish to give up or sacrifice.

It will not be unreasonable to suggest that his eventual decision to return to India at the end of World War II was, to some extent, dictated by various developments taking place all around him. On his various visits to India, he had formed a fairly precise idea of the cultural and political temper of the country. When he came out with his *Apology for Heroism* in 1946, this much had become clear to him by then that the political scene was changing. Whether it would also lead to the partition of the country or not could not be visualised at that time.

The way things were changing, it was clear to Anand that the earlier imperial dominance of India was no longer tenable. In the Apology, he described his position as "a jigsaw puzzle of my Indian upbringing and my Euro-Asian experience".

It was no coincidence that it was at this point of time that he wrote the book which he entitled, *Apology for Heroism: A Brief Autobiography of Ideas*. This book is crucial for an understanding of Anand. At one place, while talking of his decision to come to UK, he says somewhat tellingly that, "after realizing I should die or disintegrate if I could not satisfy my curiosity for truth, I left India at last in the autumn of 1925".

What he encountered in Britain has been briefly described already. At the personal level, what was happening to him was a reflection of the way his mind was evolving. Soon after his return from India in 1939, he married a British actress, Kathleen van Gelder, who was beginning to be known. They had a daughter but after a few years the marriage began to turn sour. Can it be said that it was for this reason that he thought of returning to India? In other words, could his decision to return to India be linked to his failing marriage? It is not possible to return a clear answer to this question. At any rate, everything that was happening led to a situation where returning to India seemed to be the obvious thing to do.

At this stage, it would be relevant to quote from his book, *'Apology for Heroism'*, about one thing which had shaped and conditioned the kind of writing that he was doing. What he says below is the outcome of prolonged and intensive thinking. Even the slight touch of defensiveness in what he says is not without meaning. Explaining his position, he writes:

> I could not, of course, sense the suffering of the poor directly because I had always been comparatively better off. No, mine was secondary humiliation, the humiliation of seeing other people suffer. I do not know to what extent envy of the rich on my part was disguising itself as a hunger for social justice. Perhaps there was an element of this. Also the inadequacies of our life in India may have contributed something to our preoccupation. But I do not apologise for this, because it is not easy in the face of such wretchedness and misery as I had seen in India to believe that material happiness and well being had no connection with real happiness and the desire for beauty. So I thought of the India in which I grew up, with a view to rediscovering the verities, the vapidities, the conceits and the perplexities with which I had grown up, indifferent to the lives of people around me. I felt guilty, for needless suffering was no matter for complacent

> pride or gratitude.

If it may be said, this was a fairly accurate description of his state of mind during those years.

The war years must have been a period of considerable emotional strain and turmoil for him. Though his earlier difficulties had been overcome to a large extent and he was accepted as a radical writer who had substantial literary standing, he was faced with the problem of having to come to terms with what was happening around him. Except for a few enlightened souls, the rest were not prepared to see India's point of view. India was opposed to fascism as much as any one (anyone) else in UK was. But India was not prepared to fight a war where her own future would remain undefined or uncertain. India wanted to be freed of British domination but hardly any one (anyone) in England was prepared to see India's point of view as a problem which required sympathetic and urgent attention.

Throughout the war, the situation remained undefined for India. At certain levels, it was even hostile. Meanwhile, he had got married and had family responsibilities. The war time situation made things difficult and Anand did a few odd jobs, adult teaching for instance, to support himself. It was fortunate that he had made a name for himself as a writer with the result that, as stated earlier, the BBC wanted him to take part in its anti-fascist programme. Commenting upon his relations with British intellectuals, he said, at one stage, about the contemporary dilemma:

> I was also firmly convinced that there could be no dignity in the personal relations of British and Indian intellectuals unless British writers realised that the freedom of speech and opinion which they took for granted was denied to their friends (in India) and unless they saw to it that intellectuals everywhere enjoyed equal rights of citizenship.

This was sharply put and this would not have endeared him to some of those with whom he was interacting most of the time. In his book, *Letters on India,* Anand had taken the position that while the British intellectuals accused the German fascists of all kinds of crimes, they did not apply the same yardstick to what they were doing in India.

Estrangement from most of those with whom he worked and tension with some of them was one source of his unhappiness. Another factor, though not articulated all that openly, was also at work. After almost two decades of stay in UK, his perception of India rested mainly upon his earlier memories. He had paid several visits to India, and at least one of them had lasted almost a year. Therefore, he could be said to be in touch with things in India. But being in touch with one's country was one thing and being involved with what was happening or could happen was another. To put it bluntly, his sense of belonging to India was under serious strain. This conflict between his sense of his roots in India and what he was doing in UK presumably made him take the final decision to return to India, He did so as soon as the war ended.

Since the springs of his creativity were beginning to run dry, he decided to adopt a new line of action. His interest and involvement in the study of art had been one of his strong, even obsessive, passions. On return to India, he wished to pursue the plan that he had worked out in his mind for a long time. It was a turn of good fortune that he was able to interest some of the more committed and influential people in India in this plan of his to launch a new journal. That India needed something like it also seemed obvious.

Fortunately, almost everything now fell in place as he had planned, and the first issue of *Marg* came out in 1946.

This succession of developments happened before India became self governing. This fact had no direct impact upon what he had planned or what he was doing. But the fact that it came about through a combination of circumstances in which Pandit Nehru, JRD Tata and Homi Bhabha were involved was a fortuitous coincidence. That this happened in the beginning of this phase in his career when his restless energy and creativity could not find expression in the manner he had dreamed about made it doubly fortunate. What was started in 1946 is still continuing. What is remarkable is that its impact and quality both have remained undiluted as well as undiminished.

One can go further and say that India, once she became independent and self governing, was at a stage of development when rediscovering her past was very much a part of the new agenda. The promotion of handicrafts was yet another important dimension of this hitherto-dammed creativity. It received unprecedented stimulus in the years following 1947. In brief, the situation was ripe for the kind of thing that Anand had planned and which now got launched on the eve of the independence.

Hardly anything substantial has been said so far about some other dimensions of his life during the war years. Two of them do call for some notice. One was his involvement in the Bloomsbury group. The principal source for what we know about it is his book, *Conversations in Bloomsbury*. While reasonably factual, this book, as noted by most people, is a reconstruction of what had happened half a century earlier. Meanwhile, things had changed to a considerable extent. Long conversations are reproduced but not on the basis of any contemporary record which might have been kept. Anand did not maintain a diary, it seems safe to say, nor did he claim that he recorded anything, even informally, which should have become the basis for what was being reported now.

This fact is recognised by all those people who have read the book. It makes interesting reading and throws meaningful light on what was happening at that time in the British literary circles. Also, certain individuals who mattered are given the opportunity to hold forth in great detail. For instance, there are as many as four conversations with T.S. Eliot. Each one of them is meaningful in its own way but none of them throws any new light on what we know already. In brief, the book makes no additional contribution to contemporary literary history.

Nevertheless, Anand's reporting of what happened at that time reveals a good deal about the years of his maturity in London. The phase covered in that period was before the war and dealt with that aspect in his life where he was getting drawn into British literary controversies. To be more specific, this was the period of his life when he was still a student. In the ultimate analysis, perhaps his interaction with Irene was more meaningful than his casual interaction with some of the well known literary writers whom he encountered during those years.

The second factor at work was his Marxist cum humanist leanings which became a powerful force. What started happening now was his involvement in anti-fascist organizations. This became a noticeable feature of his activity at that time. To some extent, it more or less synchronised with his period of struggle for recognition. During the war years, the situation got even more complicated. In other words, the early Marxist phase of thinking contributed to his growth as a writer but did not diminish his anxieties when he was feeling somewhat isolated and marginalised in the early 40s.

One key to his state of mind during the war years lies in two factors. The first is his novel, *The Big Heart*, which he completed about this time. This novel is somewhat like his earlier novels. And yet, it is unlike them. In his earlier novels, he drew upon the fund of his past memories. In this particular case, he knew his own caste fraternity at first hand and there is an unmistakable sense of authenticity about the manner in which he depicts his goldsmith community. At the same time, he was somewhat anxious about the declining vividness of his childhood memories. No wonder he brings in something in *The Big Heart* which is more British than Indian. There were machine riots in Britain in the nineteenth century. He had read about them in detail. But it would be a bold man who can say that there were similar riots in India also. In a sense, the use of this innovation in his writing— if one may use that word— was an attempt to cover up the yawning gap in his creative imagination.

Secondly, if one may venture to say so, Anand was running out of the raw material for his fiction and the impulse to return to India could not be ignored beyond a point. He was not exactly ignored in the literary circles. His contemporaries particularly George Orwell wanted him to participate more actively in the anti-Hitler front which was getting forged than what Anand could bring himself to do. But, as explained above, he could not forget his Indian roots nor reconcile himself to the unrelenting policies of Churchill's government which was in power then. It should not be necessary to go on with these details except to refer to what he was passing through. It is his *Apology for Heroism* which records his thoughts around that time. The date of its publication, 1946, is important. By then the war had ended and he had even paid a long-delayed visit to India in the year 1945. What needs to be remembered is that the book might have been published in 1946 but it had been written earlier. Those were years of emotional turmoil and confusion for him. He was not clear in his mind as to what he wanted to do next. The visit to India in 1945 proved to be just the right thing to have happened.

4

The Publication of *Marg*

After half a century, what would Mulk Raj Anand be remembered for? Would it be for his earlier path breaking novels or his later novels or the publication of *Marg* which he edited for over three decades? It is difficult to answer this question.

If one may hazard a guess, his novels would continue to loom somewhat large on the literary horizon for the next half century. It was with the publication of *Untouchable* that he announced his entry into the world of literature, In terms of historic importance; this accomplishment will continue to be significant, particularly in respect of Indo-Anglian fiction. While many other novelists had written about India, none of them had accomplished what Anand had.

Regional languages had published many novels which were close to the ground reality. Munshi Prem Chand's well known novel, *Godan,* is an obvious example. But no one had done the same kind of thing in English. When Anand came out with *Untouchable,* he was virtually breaking new ground. That he followed it up with an equally impressive second novel within a year and called it *Coolie* reinforced the image that he wanted to project.

No one can forget that Anand had been profoundly impressed by Gandhi's thinking and sensibility. At one point of time, he described Gandhi as his anchor. In his intellectual and artistic development, Gandhi had mattered a great deal, both as a person and as a writer of fiction. Gandhi had many fads and pet ideas but Anand learnt to ignore them. However he imbibed the basic lesson which Gandhi was trying to put across. What thrilled and inspired Anand is best expressed in the following oft-reproduced comment of Gandhi:

> I will give you a talisman, whenever you are in doubt, or when the self becomes too much with you, try the following experiment. Recall the face of the poorest and the most helpless man whom you may have seen and ask yourself, if the step you contemplate is going to be of any use to him. Will he be able to gain anything by it? Will it restore him to a control over his own life and destiny? In other words, will it lead to Swaraj or self-rule for the hungry and also spiritually starved millions of our countrymen? Then you will find your doubts and your self (yourself) melting away.

Anand literally followed what Gandhi had suggested and this becomes abundantly clear from the first couple of novels referred to earlier. If the British reading public was not prepared to read what Anand wanted to convey, it is a tribute to his persistence and his faith in himself and his ideas that he managed to get published at last. Once published, the novel made a place for itself within a matter of days. Indeed Anand became a minor celebrity overnight. As time went by and as he dug deeper and deeper into the life and destiny of the poor and the oppressed, he embodied it all in his mode of imaginative thinking which demanded to be projected.

Why has so much been said about his earlier struggle and his eventual success? The answer is explicit. In historic terms, what he did was truly memorable. If Anand made an impact both in England and India and the various other languages in which he was translated, it was, to repeat, largely because of his unique sensibility and the courage to be himself. In the near future, say, the next half century or so, his literary contribution is likely to stay undimmed. It could be even longer than half a century. But perhaps it will not extend to a whole century.

Eventually, what he will be remembered for would be the historic role that he played in giving a new turn to the contemporary Indian sensibility of those who read and wrote in English. Indeed, what he might be more remembered for is his role as a critic and promoter of Indian art. In this connection, the publication of *Marg*, started in 1946, would be seen as a landmark. His role as the man who started it would be cherished forever. Nothing like that had appeared in India until *Marg* came out. Not only was it exceptionally well produced and printed, its contents were so varied and so thoroughly researched that Indian art, both ancient and contemporary, received an extraordinary degree of projection and understanding. That *Marg* still continues to run is a tribute both to Anand who conceptualised it in the first instance, and his successors who have continued to sustain it with the same degree of commitment and excellence of which the very first issue of *Marg* had given stunning evidence.

It is a pity that more than a thousand articles were published in the journal under the editorship of Anand and almost a hundred or so were written by Anand himself, but hardly any bit of that scholarly output is to be found in any other form except what is contained in *Marg*. If nothing else, there are more than 50 to 100 books which are incorporated in those thousand odd articles and are waiting to be made available.

How is it that no one in the management of *Marg* has chosen to think along these lines? It is high time that the articles are arranged under different headings and, one by one, a whole series of books are brought out. Libraries which have been subscribing to it right from the beginning are very possessive about their collection. Indeed special care is taken to preserve these early issues so that the valuable record is not lost.

That apart, the argument advanced here is that, while during the next few decades, Anand would be remembered as a novelist and short story writer, his equally valuable contribution is likely to be as an art critic. In fact, Anand had three parallel careers, as a novelist and short story writer, an art critic, and a critic of Indian society. Each one of them deserves to be remembered and valued.

What is relevant just now is to discuss his role as an art critic. Through this journal *Marg* he opened up new layers and dimensions of art appreciation. These had remained neglected for a long time. His real stature will be seen if the full range of his art criticism is brought out in the form of books, as proposed.

If his art writings have remained both unavailable and inaccessible, it is for those responsible for this state of affairs to offer an explanation for it.

In *The Bubble* which he published in 1984, one of the characters says, "I find that every philosopher imprisons me in his thoughts while I love the free flow of my insatiable feeling away from abstract ideas". Even though it is a character speaking, Anand appears to be speaking for himself in these two lines. He was certainly interested in ideas and grappled with them endlessly throughout his life and his imagination came alive mainly when he wrote fiction. There can be no doubt that when he used those words in the course of a dialogue, he was revealing his inner mind. The transition from fiction writing to gearing himself for a career in art criticism is also equally important.

At the end of the 20s, there was an impressive exhibition of Persian paintings in London. Somewhat excited, he dug into the development of Persian painting more or less from the beginning of the Christian era. Around the first millennium, the Chinese had influenced Persian painting a good deal. A little later, in the 15th century however, there appeared an outstanding painter, Bizhad, who dominated the Persian art scene for the next few centuries to come. Not only that, there was close and intimate connection between the poetry of the great Sufi masters like Hafiz, Rumi and Jami and contemporary painting, and this is widely recognised. A good deal of this was discussed in his book on Persian Painting which he published in 1930 when he was not even 30 years of age. It was a slim volume but it showed the way Anand had started preparing himself for a career in art criticism.

A couple of years later, Anand came out with another book, *The Hindu View of Art*. This book was strongly influenced by the path breaking work of Ananda K. Coomaraswamy. At that time, he was Keeper of the Indian and Oriental Collection of the Boston Museum of Pine Arts. Coomaraswamy was a Sri Lankan who played a pioneering role in the study of Indian art. Since Indian art had spread over several countries of Asia like Cambodia, Thailand, Indonesia and others, Coomaraswamy was uniquely placed to underline the point that the Hindu view of art was strongly influenced by the Hindu view of life. More than that, the Hindu art was to be found not only in temples and other holy places but also in a whole range of crafts and the objects made by unlettered workmen who had an intuitive way of embodying beauty and grace in things they made for daily use.

Another important influence on Anand was that of Eric Gill. Gill contributed a foreword on *Art and Reality* in that book on Hindu Art. Gill was a uniquely gifted master craftsman. He was also an engraver and a type designer.

Because of his background and intensive study, he had understood the role of craftsmen who were organised in guilds in the European middle age. Eventually this bit of background led Anand to a better understanding of tribal art in India of which ample evidence is to be seen in the pages of *Marg*.

During the period of his early education and the struggle to write that book on Hindu art, Anand had been all the time preparing himself for what he started doing after 1946. When the first issue of *Marg* appeared, its impact was immediate and overwhelming. Within a few years, it virtually became mandatory reading for anyone who was interested in Indian art. As is widely known, some of the people whom Anand had got to know in Bombay were renowned architects. Anand had always been interested in architecture. As Charles Correa has aptly put it, he had an instinctive understanding of architecture and design. No wonder, he took a great deal of interest in the organization which some of the architects had set up in England. The organization was called the Modern Architectural Research Society. He replaced this last word with the use of the word Group and coined the word Marg. This word also happened to be a Sanskrit word which meant showing the way. Since this group of architects had originally planned to bring out a quarterly journal about architecture, Anand persuaded his friends in Bombay to somewhat expand its scope and coverage. That is how *Marg* became a journal of architecture and the arts when it was decided to publish it from Bombay.

Planning such a journal was one thing, publishing it was another. Not only were funds required, it was equally important that the layout, printing and presentation should be of international standards. When all these ideas were floating in his mind, Anand outlined them to Homi J. Bhabha, the father of atomic research in India. Anand had been introduced to him by Jawaharlal Nehru some time earlier. When he talked to Bhabha who lived in Bombay, and they were in regular touch with each other, he put him in touch with J.N. Tata who was the head of the Tata organization. Tata not only blessed the idea but ensured two other things.

The first one was that, as suggested by Anand, the Tata Trust undertook to advertise up to 12 pages per issue. Anand did not want anyone to control *Marg* and this was his way of doing it in terms of actual organisation. He wanted *Marg* to be autonomous and independent. In order to put him at ease regarding the fact of ownership, the Tata's agreed to advertise up to a certain number of pages in each issue. In a way, this would become a form of subsidy to the journal. This was agreed to. The second was that the Commercial Printing Press, which later on became the Tata Press, agreed to extend credit facilities, as and when necessary. As a matter of fact, everything went along favourably as visualised.

The next question was how to constitute the Editorial Board. All these details were handled by Anand. He involved architects, art historians, academics, art lovers, and several other people who had a genuine understanding of Indian art and were widely known for it. Karl. J. Khandalvala became the Art Advisor and Anil de Silva became the Assistant Editor. A word about Anil would be in order here. She was the daughter of a minister of Sri Lanka or

Ceylon as it was known then. Anand had met her in London some time earlier. She was enthusiastic about the project. Over the years, she had drawn exceptionally close to Anand. It had so happened that she along with her sister had come to Bombay and presumably rented a flat in Colaba. Both Anand and Anil became so close to each other that, before long, Anand moved to that flat and they started living together. Eventually, that Colaba address became his permanent address in Bombay.

It was after *Marg* had got going and India had become independent that Anand decided to go back to England in order to get divorce from his wife. The understanding between Anand and Anil, it appears, was that they would get married after the former had got a divorce from his wife. Anand acted as planned though it took him a little longer to get the divorce and come back to Bombay. He looked forward to his marriage with Anil only to discover on his return that she had meanwhile changed her mind and opted to marry a Frenchman. This shocked him deeply and he had some kind of a breakdown. Fortunately, he recovered from it soon after, and *Marg* began to grow from strength to strength.

The first issue which came out had a long article on Mohenjo-daro, the first Harrapan city in the Indian subcontinent. It has been dated to something like 3000 B.C. Until the city was discovered, Taxila was regarded as the most representative city of ancient Indian history which had figured even during the invasion of India by Alexander, the Great. This long article gave an exhaustive account of the discoveries going back to several thousand years before Christ. There was an article on Amrita Shergill and another on Jamini Roy. Also, there were articles on the industrial town of Jamshedpur and how to build a worker's colony and so on. One article was titled *Architecture and You*.

Anand wrote an editorial on *Planning and Dreaming*.

The production and get up were superb in every respect, and everything was highly readable and, no less important, addressed both the expert and the common man. *Marg* introduced another unique innovation. All those who advertised had to accept the format of the text as worked out by those members of the staff who worked for *Marg*. In other words, even the advertisements published in *Marg* maintained the same high level of design and production as the contributed articles. The range of articles was comprehensive and the content all inclusive.

There was no aspect of Indian art which had not been covered. Crafts like pottery and metal casting were included for purposes of analysis right from the beginning. As suggested earlier, it is astonishing that the wealth of contents made available in each issue was so comprehensive and varied. As to the authors, there was not a single name which had made a mark in the field of art criticism or had made any notable contribution and was not involved with *Marg,* Not only that, there were special theme numbers. Topics like Ellora and Ajanta art, Bharata Natayam or the Erotic Art of Konarak were covered more than once. Each issue, as Anand put it once, was an encyclopaedia in instalment.

Whether *Marg* lived up to this self-defined objective or not is illustrated best of all by the message which Indira Gandhi, the Prime Minister, sent in 1971 when *Marg's* silver jubilee was being celebrated. She wrote: Congratulations to *Marg*. It is hard to believe that this fine periodical is already celebrating its silver jubilee. Along with many others, I look forward to its issues for it brings a breath of fresh air and opens windows to diverse aspects of art—as a conscious creation and as an integral part of the daily lives, religious traditions, and festivals of our rural and other folk. In these twenty-five years. *Marg* has come to occupy a unique place amongst Indian journals. It has helped students of art in our country and abroad to evaluate the range of our art experience. It has created an awareness and appreciation amongst the uninitiated by giving them an insight into the rich and vast art treasures of our country.

A few more things require to be mentioned here. One of them is whether the publication of *Marg* was a part of an overall plan on the part of Anand or the end product of a combination of circumstances which came together at that particular point of time.

It is not possible to return a spontaneous answer to this question. Anand was not only a writer of novels and short stories or only an art critic or a keen student of contemporary Indian society. He was a combination of all three, and throughout his life he never got tired of playing any one or a combination of these roles. It is another matter that, towards the end, he became somewhat repetitive and did not always have new things to say. This becomes particularly noticeable in respect of the last phase of his fiction. Hardly any book dealing with his craft or the thematic content of his novels refers to the crop of novels which he brought out in the last decade or so of his life. Almost each one of them goes over the same ground which he had covered earlier. As to his art criticism, he would write some occasional piece but, when his connection with *Marg* got severed, he had no readymade forum of expression. As to the actual details of his social and other writings, those will be discussed later.

In other words, what needs to be reiterated is the fact that the publication of *Marg* came at a stage of his development when his grip over the Indian reality on which he had based his early fiction had begun to weaken. Therefore, he had to map out an alternative for himself. He could have stayed on in UK but more or less as a cultural exile from India. If he returned to India, as he eventually did, he had to have an alternative plan of action.

Another fact also needs a mention here. Around the time he was struggling for recognition as a writer who had something new to say, he discovered Marx. This was some kind of a turning point in his mental growth. In this connection, the best thing to do is to quote from his Apology where he has summed up this issue in these words:

> I had came to socialism through Tolstoy, Ruskin, Morris and Gandhi, imbued with the sense of this doctrine as the embodiment of an ethical creed, in so far as it was a protest against misery, ugliness and inequality. So like many of my generation, I accepted Marxism as a fairly good historical yardstick but considered humanism, the view of the whole man, as the more comprehensive ideology.

What he regarded as admirable in Marxism was the striving of the individual to "create freedom for himself within a coercive system", as a critic once put it. These ideas of his found expression neither in his fiction nor in the main body of his art criticism but mainly in political action. For a decade or more after his return to India, he remained involved in the activities of peace movement and several other initiatives promoted by Pandit Nehru.

Once *Marg* got going and he got more and more involved, he moved to Chandigarh as the Tagore Professor of Tine Arts. Partly social preoccupations, partly political activity and partly his involvement with Marg kept him going. No wonder creative writing did not (delete 'not') receive as much attention as it had been receiving earlier. However, it must be acknowledged that his role as the man who overcame the British resistance to the advent of contemporary India as one of the acceptable literary themes began to receive greater critical attention than before. And, he started paying more and more attention to the projection and display of Indian art.

What happened next was unfortunate. JRD Tata had both blessed and supported the idea of *Marg*, but the administrative set up within the Tata organization started changing with the passage of time. JRD Tata got more and more involved in his business affairs and the cultural activities undertaken by the Tata Trust came to be increasingly looked after by other members of the Trust. Before long, these individuals began to take much greater interest in the affairs of *Marg* than Anand had been accustomed to till then or, more precisely, was prepared to accept. Nothing very specific happened and there was no confrontation with anyone. But Anand began to feel somewhat uncomfortable with the kind of intrusive interest that was beginning to be taken by some of them who handled cultural matters of the Tata Trust.

What has been stated so far is not documented anywhere. The only two people who knew what was happening are no longer alive. One was Anand himself and the second was Dolly Sahiar. In saying this I am relying heavily on my memory and some speculation.

Regardless of how it happened, it is important to recognise that it jolted Anand considerably. He had sought help from the Tata's to ensure editorial independence of judgement. That did not get undermined at any stage. But some of the things that were happening must have disturbed him to a certain extent and he decided to step down. In other words, though nobody asked him to step down, he sensed changes in the work ethos and decided to withdraw.

But, did this decision eventually have a negative impact on the editorial policy of the journal or did the Tata commitment to *Marg* get diluted is a bone of contention. It can be claimed though that after some initial uncertainty, things picked up again. *Marg* is running successfully as well as productively even today. India required something like Anand's constructive imagination and sense of commitment as also the support of the Tata Trust to make this enterprise possible in the year 1946.

The Impact of *Marg* When India had been partitioned into two countries, Lahore had been allocated to Pakistan. That city had substantial non-Muslim population but when it came to division between the two countries, Amritsar (partly because of the location of the Golden Temple there) was allocated to India and Lahore was allocated to Pakistan.

Interestingly enough, Amritsar too had substantial Muslim population. All towns in what came to be called East Punjab had large concentrations of Muslims in the cities, and Amritsar was no exception. The partition of Punjab was, therefore, equally painful both for Muslims and non-Muslims, if it may be added.

The more relevant issue is that Lahore which was the capital of the undivided Punjab continued to be the capital of West Punjab. In that sense, hardly any disruption in the administrative life of Pakistani Punjab had been caused. But there was not a single city in East Punjab which could be right away declared as the capital of the new state. No wonder, Indian Punjab remained undecided about the location of its capital for quite some time. Meanwhile, Shimla was designated as the capital of the state, largely on the ground that it used to be the summer capital of the undivided Punjab. In any case, this was a stop gap arrangement. A goodly part of the rehabilitation matters were, by and large, handled at Jallandhar (Jalandhar), mainly because of its relatively accessible location. This arrangement lasted for almost a decade. By then, those who had been uprooted had settled down and things had become more or less normal.

During the first couple of years, nobody thought of building a new capital. Chandigarh did not exist at that time and it took a certain leap of imagination on the part of the Punjab government (backed by Pandit Nehru's vision of new India) that it was decided to build a new city. Anand played quite a role in the state of Punjab coming to this decision.

P.N. Thapar, a senior and influential ICS official, raised the matter with Anand at one stage. The latter said without any hesitation, "Why not build a new capital? " Hardly anybody had thought of such a thing till then. In subsequent years, a couple of other Indian states, Orissa and Gujarat for example, built their new, respective capitals. Till the beginning of the 50s, however, such an idea was regarded as much too daring.

There was a problem about where to locate the new capital. If at all a new township was to be built, it had to have room for expansion also. There was very little open space available on the main railway line running from Amritsar to Delhi. Chandigarh was located on the Ambala Kalka railway line and was considered to be a deviation from the heart of Punjab. The matter remained under discussion for quite some time and it was only after a couple of years that it got finalised. As far as one can see, Anand was not involved in any of the administrative details but he played a decisive role when it came to the selection of who was to design and plan the town. To some extent, the two issues were linked with each other.

Once, however, it had been decided to build a new capital town, the choice of the man who was going to plan it became crucial. Anand played a leading role in this respect. He put forward the name of Le Corbusier, the French architect, as the man who should be asked to do the job although it was not certain that he would accept the offer. He had so many other commitments that it virtually required a certain amount of effort to persuade him to accept the offer. What clinched the issue was the fact that almost every other project that he had undertaken had generally involved his designing a building or two. In this case, he had the freedom to plan a whole, new city.

Anand himself took the initiative to persuade Le Corbusier to accept the offer. It goes without saying that this was done after due authorization by the Punjab government and the encouragement of Pandit Nehru. He did not know Le Corbusier personally but he had heard glowing things about him from his friends connected with the field of architecture when he was in London. What was relevant now was the fact that he knew something about this innovative architect who was a brilliant personality and an equally brilliant architect with innovative ideas. After being authorised to do so, Anand called upon Le Corbusier during his next visit to Paris. As already mentioned, an arrangement was worked out to involve him both in the concept and the planning of the new enterprise.

Once the details were finalised, Maxwell Fry and Jane Drew who had worked with Le Corbusier at one time agreed to spend some time in Chandigarh. The third important member of the team was Pierre Jeannert who had been Le Corbusier's partner at one time for several years. While Le Corbusier was designated as the planner-in-chief, the other associates spent more than two years in working out the details of what had been conceptualised by Le Corbusier. To start with, the city was designed for a population of 1.5 lakhs but a provision was made for its expansion so as to be able to accommodate a population of 5 lakhs. Despite the various problems that came up later, this is how it eventually worked out. The city, even today, does not have a population of 5 lakhs but subsequent political developments have led to the establishment of two new substantial suburbs. The stamp of Le Corbusier's impact is unmistakable in each case.

One has only to refer to some of the earlier issues of *Marg* to see that, Chandigarh received a good deal of attention in every possible way. Anand himself bestowed a good deal of attention to all that was involved in building the new town. In a special issue which Marg brought out in late 1961, Anand wrote an editorial on *A New Planned City*. In order to strengthen his argument, he referred to two earlier planned cities in recent Indian history. One was Fatehpur Sikri which Akbar the Great had built and the second was Jaipur which had come up under the inspiring leadership of Sawai Man Singh. Anand focused on certain important features in each case and attempted to link up with what was under construction now. The entire planning team helped in designing the special issue. All sketches used in this issue were done by Le Corbusier himself.

Having said all this, it may not be out of place to add here that with the publication of *Marg* from Bombay, Anand spent the bulk of his time in that city. Apart from everything else, he undertook a lot of travelling both within India and in the neighbouring countries. Countries which had been influenced by Indian art received priority attention but quite a few others also received considerable attention. After about a decade, Anand organised a road trip to Europe. This meant travelling through Afghanistan, Iran, Turkey and a good many other countries. Most of what he gathered from his visit was published in *Marg* from time to time.

Apart from his involvement in the Chandigarh project, Anand was intimately involved with what eventually came to be called the Greater Bombay Scheme. In the first issue of Volume II (which came out in 1947), there was an article by Otto Koeingsberger dealing with the proposal to expand Bombay. Actually, the proposal to do so have been mooted even before the Second World War began. During the war, the city kept on expanding at a pace even greater than before.

Some of the foreign experts, either on their own or on

invitation, got involved in planning the next cycle of developments. It took some time for those developments to reach a stage when the issue of Greater Bombay moved centre stage. In a city with such a large population and limited availability of land, the issue of future planning could not but become somewhat controversial and even excite passions. Also, a good deal of big money had got unavoidably involved. In any event, from the angle of town planning, it was a major undertaking and was bound to influence thinking in respect of whatever else was being done in this area of development. It was as a part of this controversy that one entire issue of *Marg* was devoted to Planning for Bombay. Anand himself wrote an article, entitled *Splendor and Miseries of Bombay*. It went back to the East India Company days when the island of Bombay had been handed over by the Portugese (Portuguese) to the British as a part of a marriage gift. It is a detailed article and traces the rise and development of the city. In addition, there are contributions by a couple of experts and copious extracts from the Plan as drawn up by the Municipal Corporation of Bombay.

The main focus of the special *Marg* issue lay in the insightful inputs of three leading town planners. In his article on *Mulk Raj Anand at 100,* published in the book *Mulk Raj Anand: Shaping the Indian Modern,* edited by Annapurna Garimella, Correa has given a detailed description of how this act of collaboration between *Marg* and these three committed architects was undertaken. Anand himself was deeply committed to what was proposed and made no secret of where he stood. The editorial of that special issue was titled *In Dreams Begin Responsibility*.

Anand was completely professional in his approach. That did not exclude intervening in the subsidiary debates which were arising, provided it could be ensured that the overall plan was discussed objectively and professionally and in relation to what was consistent with the resources and needs of the country. In this case, the city of Bombay had grown in line with its earlier legacy and was now required to expand in the progressive manner it was now visualised.

The city has now expanded in that direction in a fairly planned manner and, in terms of transport, an appropriate railway connection and all other infrastructural facilities have been provided. While expansion had been taking place, there were some other developments also. Everything cannot be talked about in detail here except to bring to notice the fact that the process of planning got indisputably politicised over the years; As a result, some of the assumptions made earlier had to be given up. Despite these ups and downs, professional planning and the westward expansion of the city opened up new vistas for development.

Marg did not choose to discuss these subsequent developments except marginally because Anand did not stay with Marg long enough to deal with the issues that were gaining ground. Or possibly because the matters had got over-politicised. Once Anand's connection with Marg got severed, those connected with it later did not perhaps have the same kind of active involvement in the project as Anand had.

It may not be out of place to say that after Anand ceased to have any connection with *Marg,* things more or less continued as before except that in the new situation nobody planned in an organised or creative way. Things continued as before and there was no compromise with the standards of performance and production. But no one gave thought to planning and diversifying it further.

Some indication of the working of his mind during those years can be seen in a book which he brought out in the early 50s. This was called Lines Written to an Indian Air. He put together 16 essays in this book in which he attempted to analyse those aspects of Indian art and culture which required to be put at the centre of things.

While writing this book, he went beyond the parameters of what he had covered in his *Apology for Heroism* which he had written and published in England before he returned to India for good in 1945. Among the problems which he covered were those relating to literature, painting, sculpture, architecture, education, radio, cinema, women and youth. All of them could not be covered in Marg but Anand had dealt with several of them at one stage or another.

This book of his marks a stage in his intellectual development, although it is out of circulation today. Here he talks as someone who has felt deeply concerned about the faltering cultural legacy of the country and how it has been languishing for a long time. His role as a public intellectual received a sharper definition after its publication.

As mentioned already, it was open to Anand to have stayed on in London and written both about India and her society, the unfolding political turns and twists and also about her art and culture. Several people were doing this kind of analysis from a distance. But Anand's make up was different. He was both a novelist and a short story writer and also a student of Indian art. While Indian art could be studied from a distance, it was not possible to write about Indian life and society if he had remained away from India. His understanding of Indian life was beginning to diminish owing to his absence from India. If he had to ensure his future as a novelist, it was imperative for him to return and renew his intimate understanding of what it meant to be an Indian. In political terms too, the end of the war had created a situation where things were no longer the same as they used to be. This is not to suggest that he could foresee the process of the transfer of power to India and the partition of the country that somehow became an inseparable part of what was happening. All that one can say is that things were changing and he wanted to be in tune with them. This meant that he should return to India.

His several visits to India during the two decades that he had stayed in London had kept him in touch with the happenings there. Not only that, he met a large number of talented Indians who, like him, had gone to UK for education. Several of them eventually became his close friends. Quite a few of them were connected with Bombay. When he returned to India and developments of various kinds took place more or less at a dizzy speed, he could not settle down in Lahore as he had originally planned. Bombay now became the centre of his activities and it was here that he chose to settle down. The publication of Marg provided the occasion and the starting point.

When Anand was about to reach the age of 100, the Editorial Board of *Marg* planned an issue to celebrate the occasion. Unfortunately, he passed away a few months before he completed his' century. The tribute volume, published by *Marg* was, as mentioned earlier, titled *Mulk Raj Anand - Shaping the Indian Modern*. Without something like *Marg* being born at that point of time, Anand could have lost his way. This is something that needs to be underlined.

To talk of Anand's middle fiction is to enter into slippery territory. In the earlier phase which lasted till his final return to India in 1945, Anand wrote mainly about the core issues of social disparities, feudal exploitation, and the atmosphere of intimidation and flattery that had begun to flourish as one of the unsavoury outcomes of the British occupation of India. He had witnessed the process at work with his own eyes during his childhood. Life in a British army cantonment was just the setting for it.

While the process of India's conquests had gone on for more than a century and culminated in the annexation of Punjab in 1849, the rest of India had come under British rule by then. This is not the occasion to go into how British power spread from one part of the country to another. We are more concerned with the character of that impact which had been making steady inroads into Indian psyche and the results it had produced. Punjab may have been the last part of India to be taken over by the British but the eventual outcome was about the same as elsewhere.

With the passage of time, a new class of people (generally referred to as the middle class now) came into existence. To some extent, there was an alliance between this class and the feudal order. At the same time, the middle class also became the starting point of discontent against the British occupation of India. Before long, this class developed unconcealed admiration for the kind of liberal democracy that the British had built for themselves in their own country. Access to the study of English language made it possible for the members of the Indian middle class to understand how the British had gone about building their country, though one of its outcomes was to impose imperial rule over India, and among other things, recast and restructure its economy in her own economic interests.

Anand's involvement with the Bloomsbury group may have been accidental but it has to be acknowledged that this was in tune with the way his mind was functioning and growing. With his remarkable powers of observation and the ability to recall the details of the earlier experience, he took a conscious decision to become a novelist even though he had been trained as a student of philosophy. Some bits of the contributory developments to this process have been discussed already. It is time now to turn to the developments, particularly two of its main features. The first one was that his creative career, though frustrated to start with, eventually led to a splendid beginning. While *Untouchable* might have been the outcome of a certain kind of planning, and even the involvement and collaboration of Gandhi might have contributed to it, the vitality of his creative craft made it abundantly clear that, with his advent, a new voice had begun to speak. This phase of his earlier experience has already been discussed.

The second development has also been referred to though concrete evidence for it is difficult to adduce. As argued earlier, several factors intervened to give a new direction to his thinking. One, he was beginning to get emotionally exhausted and the second was his enforced stay in UK during the war years. Before the war, and more particularly after his glamorous advent in the field of Anglo-Indian writing, he had made meaningful contacts with quite a few people in India during his visits before the war. It was those visits which led to his building up a string of social connections which, on his return to India in 1945, led to fruitful results. The question now was: what next? It was not entirely clear to him how to move over to the next round of activity nor was he all that clears in his mind as to what should be its direction. Certain developments intervened. One was the publication of *Marg* more or less as he had conceived it. Another was his chance encounter with the de Silva sisters whom he had met earlier in London and who had now moved to Bombay from Colombo. The elder sister was an architect but it was the younger one, Anil, who got personally drawn to him. One of the factors which led to his return to the writing of fiction was Anil's decision to leave him in favour of someone else. This resulted in an emotional crisis and he was advised to do creative writing as a form of therapy. This eventually helped him overcome the nervous breakdown that he had suffered.

He also travelled a good deal during these years. It can be claimed that, in terms of his creative output, the 50s were more or less an unproductive span of time for him. In the case of *The Private Life of an Indian Prince,* the critical opinion is divided. Most of the critics do not rate it highly. This was despite the fact that the stage for the merger of the states with the Indian Union during the years after 1947 was a burning topic of discussion and was very much a part of the contemporary political agenda. If Anand chose to write on the private life of an Indian prince, it was more or less in tune with what most people were talking about.

Before he left for UK, Anand had spent some time in Shimla. During this period he had worked as a tutor to a couple of small princes. This dimension of life was therefore not unfamiliar to him in other words, when he chose to write on this theme, Anand was writing about something which he had known at first hand. Despite these favourable factors, most readers are critical of this particular novel. For one thing, it was unlike his earlier novels where the heroes were invariably victims of the social forces at work. For another, he had dignified them by making them the leading characters of his novels and by taking up their crisis situation as the core issue. To be precise, in writing the kind of novels that he wrote in that phase of his career, Anand had broken new ground.

Writing about the princes was to some extent the obverse of what he had been doing so far. The only notable critic who has said anything positive about this novel is Saros Cowasjee. In his edited volume, Mulk Raj Anand Omnibus, published by the Penguins after Anand's death, apart from *Untouchable* and *Coolie*, this is the third novel to be included. Cowasjee has described it as the most "profound" of Anand's novels. According to him, "by focusing upon the principal characters of the novel—*Vicky and Ganga Dasi*—these characters are described as individuals of such complexity and with such psychological insight that critics will go on redefining them".

Anand wrote this novel in the background of his

own emotional crisis. To what extent this fact came in the way of his writing an acceptably good piece of fiction is difficult to say. The fact remains that if Anand is remembered today as a novelist, it is not because of this or other novels but *Untouchable* and *Coolie,* which have been included by Cowasjee in his Omnibus volume. What is more significant, however, is that, in terms of his creative output, the decade of the 50s was comparatively barren as far as Anand was concerned.

Anand's autobiographical novels fall into a special category, if one may say so. *Seven Summers* had, by and large, been shifted from the 2,000-page long autographical account of his past that he had written for himself under the inspiration— or whichever way we put it—of his friend, Irene. He kept on pouring out the details of his childhood and the subsequent years to her. She was fascinated by what he was telling. Before long, he reduced it to writing and, little by little, it became a manuscript of almost 2,000 pages. Irene did him the favour of typing them out, and the manuscript became the potential source material for some bits of what he wrote later. Apart from this particular feature of *Seven Summers,* a notable quality of this novel is a certain kind of freshness about it. This feeling of freshness comes from a variety of sources. One is the mood of effortless ease which it conveys. Another is the kind of child that he was - irrepressibly curious, always willing to experiment and to learn and adjust. Anand depicts the child as one whom he cannot but project in any way other than with genuine warmth and sincerity.

As Anand himself says somewhere, an autobiographical novel is not the same thing as an autobiography. The distinction is important and has to be kept in mind while discussing these novels. Even though he intended to write an autobiography, he never got around to doing so except incidentally. In a pamphlet put out by his publisher, even the title of each of the seven volumes of the proposed series was given. It was envisaged that, on the lines of *Seven Summers* and others, three more novels would be written. Those were listed as *So He Played His Part, A World Too Wide,* and *The Last Scene*.

Only the first four got written and the other three remained unwritten or, maybe, he changed his mind or whatever. There was one exception which will be dealt with a little later. One other was that he wrote a small book titled *Little Plays on Mahatma Gandhi*. This slim volume was published and circulated but did not measure up to the earlier volumes.

The point is that perhaps owing to his other preoccupations or a change of plan, the autobiography was not written. In addition to the one referred to above, the other three autobiographical novels that were published were *Morning Face, Confessions of a Lover,* and *The Bubble*. There was also a further confusion in respect of planning the series of autobiographical novels.

In his eventual approach, he does not stick to either of these approaches with the result that there is a certain degree of ambiguity about the whole thing. Even when one overlooks all this confusion, the fact remains that each one of the novels needs to be evaluated in its own right. This is for the simple reason that he was not consistent in his planning or approach nor always consistent in the execution of what he had planned.

How does Anand come across? Of his childhood, this much is indisputable that he was curious and even precocious to some extent. He was all the time asking all kinds of questions. While some of them were answered, others were not but each one projected a new dimension and level of understanding. As a child, he was extremely fond of his mother and was somewhat afraid of his father.

In addition to the fact that he received boundless love from his mother, one thing that endeared his mother to him particularly was her gift for storytelling. In this connection, his own words given in the novel may be quoted here:

My mother had a vast fund of folk tales, having heard them in her childhood from her own mother, as legends, fables, myths and other narratives of gods and men and birds and beasts have been told in endless variations for thousands of years on the flat roots of the mud huts in the villages.

As a matter of fact, his mother seems to have stimulated his imagination by telling him stories day after day. A kind of special bond grew up between them. This happens in many a home. All that one can say is that his mother was one of those exceptional women who laid the foundations of a goodly part of what he accomplished in later life. Altogether, Seven Summers makes for compulsive reading and successfully evokes the picture of a lively and curious child. And there lies the strength of this first auto-biographical novel.

5

Social Discrimination in Indian Society

In *Untouchable,* Anand describes a day in which Bakha, an untouchable who has worked for a British regiment, comes to a certain level of consciousness about casteism. That element of westernization is a necessary precondition for Bakha–he is already set apart by the bits of British clothing he wears, he plays hockey (his joining other players unaware of his untouchability is an important gear in the narrative mechanism), he has been treated differently by the regiment than by those who know him "back home," he has acquired more desires than he can pay for, he has westernized shame over the spitting and hawking in Indian ablutions–he has, we read, invented a new world out of these traces of a different order:

He didn't like his home, his street, his town, because he had been to work at the Tommies' barracks and obtained glimpses of another world, strange and clean; he had grown out of his native shoes into the ammunition boots that he had secured as a gift. And with this and other fashionable items of dress, he had built up a new world, which was his heaven, if for nothing else, because it represented a change from the old classified order and the stagnant pools of the lane near which he was born.

This imagined world does not mesh seamlessly with that of the town, and the novel works by giving us the interior responses of Bakha to scenes which dramatize the gap between Bakha's worlds.

Anand takes no chances with reader's sympathies: the novel operates a simple binary mechanism pitting a favorably marked Bakha against all others' defects or brutality. Not only is Bakha dramatized as a "lion", but many passages mark his strength, nobility, and inherent dignity. Moreover, many incidental traces of caste walls explain daily life from his perspective (caste-bound wells, his regret over exclusion from education, the "sin" of an untouchable presuming to smoke, the difficulty of shopping when you can't touch or be touched, his ignorance even of religion because of being banned from temples, the taking up by many Brits of caste prejudices, the difficulty of moving along a street without touching or being touched). We witness extreme examples of prejudice–high caste jokes at Bakha's clothes and cleanliness, women's abuse of untouchables at a well, venomous language over untouchables' request for a raise or simply for walking normally instead of skulking, blame and abuse for defiling a hurt boy he carries home from the hockey field.

By taking us inside Bakha's emotional life, we are invited to identify with a type of whom Anand's first readers had no deep knowledge. We have, for example, the story of the regimental hat all the Indian boys covet. "The spirit of modernity had worked havoc among the youth of the regiment", particularly the "desire to wear western dress." For Bakha, it has always been the hat, so intensely so that he had once, as a boy, asked for it, but in his maturity could not bring himself to.

> 'Why is it,' he had often asked himself, 'that I can't go and ask now but dared to do so when I was a child?' He couldn't find the answer to this. He didn't know that with the growth of years he had lost the freedom, the wild, careless, dauntless freedom of the child, that he had lost his courage, that he was afraid.

This brief passage is a microcosm of the contradictions Bakha experiences among youth and age, westernized and untouchable, emergent and constrained, and it shows as well how dependent Anand is upon the powerful engine of individualism to enlist sympathies and arouse passion. Anand juxtaposes a westernized self–a utopian ideal even in the west, one free of all markers of class, gender, and ethnicity–with the constructed Indian self of an untouchable.

The juxtaposition is not without its difficulties. Note for example this description of his neighbors whom Bakha considers "inferiors" from his westernized perspective:

A few other outcastes were busy killing lice from the pleats of their shirts and trousers and too comfortable in the sun to bother to look up. As they sat or stood in the sun, showing their dark hands and feet, they had a curiously lackadaisical lazy, lousy look about them. It seemed their insides were concentrated in the act of emergence, of a new birth, as it were, from the raw bleak wintry feeling in their souls to the world of warmth. The taint of the little prison cells of their one-roomed homes lurked in them, even in the outdoor air. They were silent as if the act of liberation were too much for them to bear....

The tone is menaced by the difficulty of showing the degrading effects of housing without being tinctured by the superiority Bakha feels as he walks into the settlement.

A similar danger surfaces in the depiction of Bakha listening to the speeches of Christians, Gandhians, and the poet of technology. The Christians are simply skewered, when the Colonel seeks paternally to save "the souls of the heathen" or we see the blunt racism ("these blackies") of his wife. But Bakha's limitations are also made explicit, presumably to register the extent to which his intellectuality has been stunted, but in terms that risk even more than the description of the "lazy, lousy" outcastes: Bakha "followed willingly," we read, "listening to each word that the Colonel spoke, but not understanding a word" . Listening to the Gandhians, Bakha is befuddled by the unknown word "harijan", he "looked not unlike an ape as he sat" watching the procession, and he "didn't understand these words" of Gandhi (words like moral, religious, conscience). And the anti-Brahminical poet who rants after the Mahatma's speech fares no better, for though he advances technology as the cure to the untouchables' dilemma and urges Indians to pick and choose among western traits, Bakha "felt that the poet would have been answering the most intimate questions in his soul, if he had not used such big words". Anand marks the most thoroughly failed sense of solidarity with the masses by having Mr Bashir, a Jinnah-like aristocrat paired with the poet, flourish his "silken handkerchief" as he detaches them from a crowd that has "suffocated" him.

Perhaps Anand is not entirely immune to the list of sins we laid at Forster's feet, but it is the containment within a westernized individualist ethic that is most worrisome. We see Bakha register bodily the anxiety produced by these alternative conceptions of his group, flushed, fast-pulsed, and confused, and we leave him "torn between his enthusiasm for Gandhi and the difficulties in his own awkward, naive self". Anand's book is to set an agenda, it seems, in which treatments of the untouchables risk eviscerating the need for structural change with the emphasis upon the individual psyches of their protagonists, reintroducing, along the way, trace elements of the privileged position from which the writing comes.

But let us fast-forward to a novel published a few years after the revised edition of Anand's *Untouchable*, when the Gandhian term, harijan, becomes the title of Shanta Rameshwar Rao's *Children of God* (Bombay: Sangam Books, 1976). Perhaps the most striking thing about this South Indian narrative is how continuously its key points parallel not only Anand's 1935/1970 novel, but also a 1991 journalistic report on *The Awful Truth: Continuing Oppression of Harijans in Tamil Nadu* (in *Aside: The Magazine of Madras*, 15 March 1991), and the 1988 *Pan on Fire: Eight Dalit Women Tell Their Story* (New Delhi: Indian Social Institute). Perhaps only western readers would notice this continuity, expecting otherwise given the rapid changes in our own social surfaces over the last few decades. But a century is a short stretch of time in which to touch this bottom line of caste with a magic wand of Equity. As if to buttress the point of continuity despite agitations for change, many of Rao's sociological moments occur also in these other narratives– the rude mores at the village (caste) well, male alcoholism and domestic violence, child-raising attitudes, extortionary lending rates, the persistence of caste prejudice among liberals when it comes to issues of (e.g.) marriage, and a general multitude of restraints upon Dalit dress, demeanor, and movement in a traditional village. The Madras magazinist, Janaki Venkataraman, concludes that "if you are a Harijan and you live in a Tamil Nadu (or any Indian) village, you do not, in reality, possess the same fundamental rights that an average Indian citizen possesses".

That verdict casts a shadow across the century's rhetoric of equality under the law. "Right through the trip undertaken by Aside reporters in Tamil Nadu it was noticed that the law of the land stops at the panchayat tree in every village (where the most local of councils meets). There the law of the village (oor kattuppadu) takes over". That oor kattuppadu is not enforced by formal edict. Full of anecdotes about panchayat presidents pocketing half the loan money obtained under uplift schemes, land distribution scandals, the suffusion of caste lines even into the Christian churches, let alone the terms of address in the villages, the Aside account makes clear the diffuse mechanics by which old normalizing conditioning is applied:

The fact is, all law enforcing authorities are quite aware that their words or actions carry no weight within the village–there, only the word of the local landlords (usually caste Hindus) carries weight as they have the power to give or take away jobs, ban an entire community from using the amenities or services in the village and unleash violence.

Indeed, Bihar, for example, is notorious for its private armies of landowner goondas who patrol the countryside despite the importance of SCs (Scheduled Castes in legal parlance) when votes are counted.

And so both Rao and the journalists tell anecdotes of old SC women removing their sandals because they aren't permitted to wear them on village streets, laws notwithstanding. All these accounts share retellings of abuse at the well, being forced to wash laundry only downstream and at night, scolding's for making eye contact or speaking directly to a caste Hindu, beatings for inadvertently touching a caste Hindu, outrage when SCs use forbidden routes in daylight, and stoning for wearing a full sari or flowers in the hair. The novel's narrator alternates between narrating her community's lifestyle and lamenting her dead son Kittu, beaten and burnt to death for entering a temple more than 25 years after Independence era legislation. All of the accounts juxtapose the rhetoric of equity with the abusive outrage of onlookers and the weary cynicism of a character like Soma: "Make no mistake! Words are like the husk of grain–empty, useless and plentiful. People give words, and that is all they have to give you".

Among those words are the arguments swirling around caste reform issues, carefully parsed by Rao during the narrator's flashbacks to the heady days of Mahatma Gandhi's campaign against untouchability. We hear angry outbursts from reactionary crowds, bus-riding Brahmins trapping reformers in classic arguments from karma and rebirth, conservative Dalits worried about the impiety of polluting the better-born, verbal assaults on foreign missionaries backing the egalitarian cause. As for the narrator, she falls in love with Acharya Harishchandra (who, perhaps caste-bound himself, doesn't even notice); The Teacher's angry denunciation of the caste bar is equitably distributed between the defenders of caste privilege and those who submit to it:

You have been called untouchable only because you have allowed men to call you and treat you as such. You have allowed yourself to be treated worse than animals, and held out your hands for the shackles that men have put upon you. Time and time again they told you that you were untouchable, and you, in your crass ignorance and simplicity believed it, and never questioned it. Do you understand? It is only because they have told you and your fathers that you are untouchable that you have believed it, and not because it is so. But if you repeat a lie a hundred times over, does that make it the truth?

We hear a middle class edge (patronizing, paternal, and viscerally attuned to markers of relative sophistication) in phrases like "crass ignorance and simplicity," a quite middle class ethos (of self-sufficient upward mobility) impacted in the verb "allowed," and an utterly (post?) modernist critique lacing through the trope of repeating a lie to impose "truth."

The splicing of narrative time in the novel is perhaps its most telling argument about equity and reality in caste politics. All the arguments about equity and equality are placed 25 years in the past; the most devastating examples of caste prejudice (brother Boda's discovery that urban liberals still harbor prejudice, Kittu's murder) take place in the present. "Chhaya," in Pan on Fire, mentions a modus operandi by which members of her family negotiate the difference between tradition and modernity: "my uncle says, at home he listens to his mother and outside he listens to his heart". The maxim applies to equity in caste matters, it would seem, with many of the protagonists of these fictional and nonfictional accounts listening to a heart of equity and principle "outside" in the public realm of rhetoric, but to the "mother" of traditional bars and prejudice in the "home" of marriage and friendship. Boda, for example, discovers this principle when his wish to marry the sister of his "friend," a liberal labor organizer, meets with silence, then outrage:

> ... you are a fool, Boda, if you do not understand that marriage is another thing altogether. ... Marriage is a bond by which a man secures himself to his family and ancestors; to the roots out of which he was created. Marriage is different. Are you so stupid as not to know that?

A bit of this sixty-year continuity erodes if one turns to writing by Dalits, speaking of, as, and for themselves. Even Pan on Fire is a curious project in which participants were first trained in techniques of autobiographical recall, and then their transcripts edited, and a final selection made and rendered into English–multiple levels of structuring and selection that fairly obtrusively construct the personae and their narratives. One can sense these participants (in a Christian-sponsored social outreach project) striving to "perform" for the workshop leaders, to foreground attitudes and events that "fit" the ethos of social services (to the point of the younger ones aspiring to become social workers themselves). The Introduction to the volume notes that role rather than individual ability shapes behavior and that, therefore, "it is the roles that shape the life experience and personality and not vice versa" as in the middle class, one might add, where a sufficient economic buffer can often vary the possibilities a bit. But one of the roles these women play is as interlocutor in a social services program that treats them as honored guests, offers some help with various life crises, and generally lifts the self-esteem of participants by making them more like the questioners than like those whose narratives were not chosen for the book.

Perhaps the Dalit writers collected in a series of anthologies by Arjun Dangle, one of the Dalit Panthers from the 1970s, are similarly constructed by their participation in literary forms that "modernize" the individuality of protagonists and writers. But a volume like *Homeless In My Land* (Bombay: Disha Books, 1992), the short story component of a series that also includes poetry and autobiography, nonetheless offers several vantage points upon Dalit life, including urban (like Boda's story in Children of God, or most of the participants in Pan on Fire's project), rural (like Bakha's story in *Untouchable* or Laxmi's in Children of God or the cases in the Madras magazine), and even a bit of the Dalit middle class, all of them reliant upon social realism to detail the situation of Dalits in this half of the century. In the urban stories, for example, we see Beehma driven to stealing "Gold from the Grave" when his quarry job disappears in a downturn (and losing his fingers in the clench of a corpse's mouth as he fights off jackals to steal rings and jewels, on the de Maupassant eve of the quarry rehiring the able-bodied). We also see a mother ostracized, even by her own son, for her liaison with the overseer, (though the son's moralistic fastidiousness contrasts sharply with women's envy of his mother and men's lust for her, as if the mob that works on the boy is mostly angry that sexual property is passing outside the community). We see a child so deformed it becomes the "Livelihood" of a woman until its father gets out of prison and exercises a father's "ownership" of children.

In each of these urban stories, the writers take pains to dramatize the collusion of other Dalits in the suffering of protagonists, an indication that these writers believe collective action is more effective than internalizing social inequity and economic disparity and venting such anger within the Dalit community. The rural stories remind one of the narratives we've discussed–stories of *Poisoned Bread* tossed to the Dalits as their traditional portion, an urban retiree's *Storeyed House* burnt (with him inside) to punish such uppitiness, a gentle boy pathetically inept at struggling for a good share in *The Cull* (when Dalits share out a dead buffalo as their compensation for disposing of a polluting dead carcass), an educated Dalit boy who cannot find employment and must return to outcaste trades to support his family. The egalitarian reform rhetoric in the plot of *Poisoned Bread* turns ironic given the 12-year retrospective narration from an unchanged present. The middle class story recounts the gap between the father's *Promotion* in the regulated hierarchy of a government department and the insolence of Godbole or with the son's wounded knee (and pride) from being pushed and beaten for drinking water in a caste house. "Waghmare's mind is filled with the image of Godbole. His newly-sprung wings of promotion fall off and a mere mortal named Pandurang Satwa Waghmare crashes helplessly into the abyss below".

That abyss is an historical past, internalized within all these characters, into which all rhetoric of liberty, fraternity, and equality must pass. Waghmare has "risen," but so insecurely that he fears any contact between his family and their relations in the chawls ("what will our neighbors say," he actually asks when his wife mentions running into her slum-dwelling aunt). That instability signifies the multiplicity of roles he must play without any warranties, manipulating the laws to raise economically, but also contending with the persistent realities of caste lines and bars fissuring the social body. Changes being brought by contemporary economic patterns open the abscess of caste feelings–in the same way that ethnic identities are more tightly held and keenly felt as media homogenization and global pricing and sourcing undermine their social texture. Impatience, even militance, is bred by relative have-nots seeing evidence of the sheer amount of stuff people have in societies with more equity (which may well only mean differently distributed inequities). While these disparities have always existed, they had been tied to partially soothing Brahminical doctrines of "one's destiny" accrued from past lives. MTV broadcasts continuous reminders that anyone can rise when equity floods out the caste lines and its (it's) supporting religious and social institutions. Intercaste rioting (prominent in both Tamil Nadu and Bihar recently) is only the extrovert form of the introverted venom evidenced in the stories Dangle collects.

It is not any easier, that is, to be a Dalit than a caste Hindu when the structures and rules begin to flow. Rao's caste Hindus can mutter that "If we do not have a care, these people will become our equals and we will have no position left," a lostness that mirrors Boda's when he arrives in Bombay:

> He had come to escape from the prison of untouchability, but the prison would not leave him and presently the thought of his untouchability began to torment him as it had never before done. Again and again he found himself wondering if he was not unwittingly committing a heinous sin by polluting so many people.

And this from a man who had been contemptuous of religion, who had defied caste lines in his village, and who had left so that the weight of unjust history would no longer be upon him. The "prison" is within as his core identity, and it comes with the "torment" of its externalized forms (in this case, religious law) and the striation of social hierarchy ("heinous" derives, appropriately in this context, from "hate"). Its discipline is the more keenly felt as he enters the City, a zone in which the daily pressure of traditional caste norms seems suspended. The persistence of its memory haunts equally the government officer in Arjun Dangle's *Promotion,* who keenly feels the risk to their new position of continuing any connections with Dalits still in the chawls–as if the new structure of class and meritocracy were a veil of illusion cast over the hard realities of karma and destiny.

Identity politics, in other words, are not a solution but a symptom of a more complex sedimentation of discontinuous and asymmetrical formations that mix social, cultural, political, and above all economic modes. The content of the Dalit case history is not invalid, but it provides an inadequate, even simplistic model for "solving" the problem. India is not a modern problem to be socially engineered with a totalizing modernist purism. It is a postmodernist pastiche with manifold mutually symptomatic structures already partially decomposed and floating in the rivers of time like a post-festival Ganapati image. "Dalit" identity, in fact any such singular identity, names too small a part of the whole of each protagonist, just as caste, religion, language, or even class names too singular a version of the social whole. Contradictory composites, they elude the monological conceptuality of modern social theory or narrative form and require a far more inclusive and mobile logic.

The Novel, as Mukherjee reminds us in the historical chapters of Realism and Reality, does stagger a bit as a genre when setting its formal encoding of individualism in relation to a communally defined social body like Indian society. We've seen the effects of three distinct waves in which this tension was articulated. In the colonial past, communities were strategically manipulated factions of a potentially mutinous colonized population, the lower orders dosed with liberally inspired aspirations that set them against a traditional elite itself dosed with carefully measured degrees of partial authority and moderate material rewards. Anand's *Untouchable* and *Coolie* exemplify such a phase. In the nationalist past, this taking of an exclusive part as a focal whole–"India" is your caste, it is Brahmanical Hinduism, it is the emerging middle class, it is the target audience of the political day–gave way, relatively and not ever altogether, to secularism's modernist dream of a single national identity, a totalizing fiction always easier to maintain from a position of privilege than from one of caste and economic subjection. Partition narratives? Surprise at the intensity of communal violence expresses their shock that this supposed nationalist homogeneity had in fact failed to wash out old boundary lines of communal ontology.

As novels begin appearing in the post-Nationalist era of post modernity, we begin to see these categories undergo yet another level of stress and strategic repositioning as the new economy and its international media shock troops break up and empty fundamental social structures and equally fundamental "modern" frames of reference like individuality and nation. In the violent flare-ups of communal anachronism, the backlash of an increasingly displaced social logic, it can be difficult to imagine how thoroughly mixed the identities of individual Indians have become: we have seen narrative after narrative unravel any simplicity to the question of "identity," sometimes in relief at the liberation from its restrictions, sometimes with nostalgia at the sense of something lost, sometimes with grim recognition of the kind of being one must assume in its place. The formula narrative that Bollywood began, SATV accelerates; the progress that Nehru preached, Rupert Murdoch has commodified; the professional class that the British initiated as a managerial strata (stratum) for a colonial regime, global capitalism has exponentiated as software development, engineering, and any number of other such technical exports. Each individual in these going concerns bears within what I've called a romance of memory, a romance of identity, while negotiating the generic postmodernity (post modernity) of Hyatt-Regency meetings and Amex gold card mobility.

We turn next to a novel in which this third scenario is in full and tragic evidence, opening out for us to a chapter on women writing about women in which we see some of the most compelling and detailed close readings of the social and personal effects of post modernity. Post modernity's deracination of social logics sorely tests the resources of both individuals and tradition itself, flexible as we have found it to be, to accommodate themselves to the drastically changed life world produced by the global economic order's wildfire spread across the social and historical landscape of India.

6

The Novels of Mulk Raj Anand

Mulk Raj Anand, a socially committed novelist, has produced a good deal of literature. He has written more than a dozen novels and about seventy short stories and a host of essays and articles on a number of subjects. His novels fall into two categories namely social and autobiographical novels. He focused his attention on the sufferings, misery and wretchedness of the poor as a result of the exploitation of the downtrodden class of the Indian society. Religious hypocrisy, feudal system, East-West encounter, the place of woman in the society, superstitions, poverty, hunger and exploitation are his common themes. The present chapter deals with five of his novels namely, *Untouchable* (1935), *Coolie* (1936), *Two Leaves and a Bud* (1937), *The Sword and the Sickle* (1942) and *The Road* (1963), which deal with poverty, hunger and exploitation as their major themes.

'Untouchable' Mulk Raj Anand's first novel *Untouchable,* published on 1st May 1935, was welcomed by a few but criticized by many. Several news-papers in London criticized

it as 'a dirty work'.

E.M. Forster anticipated such criticism in his preface to *Untouchable*. He says; it seems to me indescribably clean and I hesitate for words in which this can be conveyed. Avoiding the rhetoric and circumlocution, it has gone straight to the heart of its subject and purified it.

The novel gained popularity among the Western readers slowly but surely. The Preface written by E. M. Forster made them perceive its aesthetic value. Later it became so popular that it was translated into more than twenty languages. Saros Cowasjee in his book So Many Freedoms rightly observes:

The book however quickly cut its way through supercilious criticism and established for itself a popularity that remains unrivalled for work of fiction by any Indian author.

The novel covers the span from 1930 to 1940 when poverty, slavery and the inhuman exploitation of the masses were at the peak. It was Gandhi who had waged a war against the forces behind these evils. The novel describes a single day in the life of the protagonist Bakha, a scavenger boy. The entire action takes place within a period of less than twenty four hours. Though the scene of the novel belongs to a small, interior town of the Punjab, the happenings are pan Indian in character. Bulandshahr, a small town with an outcaste colony on the outskirts represents a normal Indian town found anywhere in India. Most of the action of the novel takes place at an outcaste colony and in the streets of the small town.

Bakha starts his day welcomed by the abuses of his father and is forced to clean the latrines with a brush and a basket. His sister Sohini goes to fetch water from the caste well where she is compelled to wait for a caste Hindu to draw water which is again a routine for her life. Pandit Kali Nath fills her pitcher with water and summons her, with an ill intention to clean the temple courtyard. Bakha, on the request of his father rushes to the town to clean the roads. On his way he meets his friends and they plan a hockey match in the afternoon.

While walking through the streets of the town, a caste Hindu gets defiled by his touch to which he tries to apologize. Joining his hands in humility, he stands deaf and dumb. The people gather around the scene and abuse Bakha. He pleads but no one feels pity for him. The defiled man gives a slap on Bakha's face and leaves the place. For the first time in his life Bakha is made aware of his status as an untouchable. He feels insolent and rushes to the courtyard of the temple announcing his arrival aloud. While roaming outside the temple he curiously looks into the temple. A Brahmin sees Bakha on the steps and shouts at him for polluting the temple. While climbing down the steps he finds his sister Sohini standing in the courtyard frightened and speechless. She tells Bakha about the priest's attempt to molest her while she was cleaning his latrine. She further tells him that she screamed out of fear and the priest came out shouting that he had been defiled by an untouchable girl. An enraged Bakha decides to look for the priest but Sohini stops him. As both of them realize their helplessness due to the limitations of their caste, they decide to give up. Bakha sends Sohini home and goes to an alley nearby to beg for food.

He starts shouting for food but nobody responds. Tired of the hectic schedule he sleeps on the wooden platform in front of a caste Hindu's house. A high caste woman comes out of the house on the call of a Sadhu. She shouts at Bakha for polluting her house. She asks him to clean the drain to get a piece of bread. Meanwhile a woman from a neighbouring house gives him a chapatti. He returns home and tells his father Lakha about his insult and Sohini's molestation by the Pandit. To assuage his son's grief Lakha narrates him a nasty experience of his own life. It brings Bakha back to his senses. He leaves the house to meet his friends. After spending some time with his friends he goes to Hawaldar Charat Singh to collect a hockey stick. Bakha gets excited with his kind treatment and goes to the playground to play a hockey match.

The son of a high caste Hindu is hurt in the quarrel that takes place after the match. When Bakha takes the wounded boy to his house, his mother, instead of giving thanks shouts at Bakha for defiling her son and the house. As he returns home in the afternoon, his father welcomes him with abuses for bunking his afternoon latrine cleaning work. Utterly given up to despair he goes out and sits under a pipal tree cursing the day. Colonel Hutchinson, a priest from the church, finds him lonely and takes him to the church where he asks Bakha to confess his sin so that he can be converted to the Christain religion. The Colonel's wife shouts at him for bringing a '*bhangi*' at her house. Bakha runs away from the church.

While wandering through the railway station he hears the news of Mahatma Gandhi's arrival in the town. He rushes to Golbagh to hear Gandhi's speech. With the sight of Gandhi he forgets all the miseries of the whole day. In his long speech Gandhi expresses his wish to be reborn as an untouchable. He calls them '*Harijan*' and the cleaners of Hindu religion. He also warns them against their bad habits and asks them to stop accepting the cooked food for their work. Through the conversation between the two pro- and anti- Gandhi groups, Bhaka comes to know that the only solution to eradicate untouchability is the use of machine or the flush system. With this Anand is the first Indian novelist to have depicted in the novel from the stigma of this evil which isolates a man from his own society.

Not only the protagonist but also most of the minor characters in his novels belong to the low caste, downtrodden society. Mulk Raj Anand in his article *The Source of Protest in my Novels* says, I wished to create the folk, whom I knew intimately, from the lower depths, the lumpens and the suppressed, oppressed repressed, those who have seldom appeared in our literature.

All these characters embody a particular vision of reality which the novelist has assigned to them. They are normal, simple, credible human beings unaware of their social condition. In the preface to Two Leaves and a Bud Mulk Raj Anand says, "All these heroes and the other men and women... were the reflection of the real people I had known during my childhood and youth.... They were the flesh of my flesh and blood of my blood." Bakha's character is modeled after one of Anand's childhood friends, who was humiliated by his own mother for being a sweeper boy but whom Anand adored as a hero. Anand could never forget that sweeper boy and the insult and humiliation that he received by Anand's family. He gave voice to his views against the exploitation of a sweeper-boy through the character of Bakha in his very first novel *Untouchable*.

According to Premila Paul, Bakha serves as a mirror to the pathetic correlation of the untouchables. He represents all those sweepers who are doomed to live life worse than the slaves. E.M. Forster in his Preface to *Untouchable* rightly observes, "...the slave may change his master and his duties and may even become free, but the sweeper is bound for ever, born into a state from which he cannot escape and where he is excluded from social intercourse".

During his psychological transition from innocence to experience, he faces identity crisis. Initially he possesses no awareness of being an outcaste. The kind treatment from the White Tommies makes him feel superior to his fellow outcastes and this superiority complex is reflected in his attitude and appearance. He does not live unclean or uncouth like other scavengers. His intelligence, sensitivity and the air of dignity differentiate him from his fellow outcastes. Even a high caste Charat Singh feels "Here was a low caste man who seemed clean". He calls Bakha a gentleman.

But his role as a gentleman is thwarted by a series of incidents that happen during a single day. He suffers without any fault of his own. The slap he receives from the high caste Brahmin for defiling him by his touch makes him aware of his true identity. Soon after this, he faces another moment of humiliation at the steps of the temple that increases the rage in his soul. But the molestation of his sister by the priest turns him violent to which he reacts aggressively. The giant stride of the sweeper towards the temple frightens the crowd. "His fist was clenched. His eyes flared wild and red, and his teeth ground between them the challenge: 'I could show you what that Brahmin dog has done!'." But his hereditary serfdom acts as a handicap to his spontaneous rebellion. He realizes that he can do no more than being enraged against the brutalities of the high castes.

Instead of appreciation, Bakha receives condemnation even when he saves the child from an accident and takes him to his home lifting on his hands. The thankless mother of the child shouts at him for defiling her house and wounding her son. He thus receives inhuman treatment from almost everybody. They throw things at him the way they do to the animals. This inhumanity reaches its climax when a so-called mother throws a thin slice of bread at him from the top of her house. He feels ashamed of himself for picking up the bread from the pavement.

He is simultaneously an exploited person and a rebel. He is a scapegoat of the rigid caste system. Injustice inflicted upon him makes him rebellious. Excessive abuse and insult makes him think about retaliation. At such moments he feels like a tiger at a bay. Saros Cowsjee in her book So Many Freedoms rightly says, But he is a tiger in a cage, securely imprisoned by the conventions his superiors have built up to protect themselves against the fury of those whom they exploit.

Bakha wants to protest but he who cleans the filth of the people becomes aware of the filth around him. He realizes that he is surrounded by his own people who are meek, humble and who have accepted exploitation as their fate. His father tries to calm him down by making him realize that such exploitation is not unknown to their caste. His sister, Sohini, also tries to pacify him by asking him to accept it as a part of their destiny. His inability to revolt should be perceived as an outcome of the oppression of the outcastes for thousands of years.

His submission to the superiors who exploit him is the result of the inborn slavery that he inherits. Bakha imitates the life style of the Whites and desires to live life in their manner. While copying the White sahib in all regards, his excessive 'fashun' makes him an object of ridicule. Some of the critics call it a colonial exploitation of Indians by the British. It is important to discover whether Bakha's imitation of Tommies is a symbolic representation of the youth in Pre- Independent India or an untouchable's natural reaction against the exploitation by the high caste Hindus. If it is considered as a symbolic representation of the youth, such a reaction was generally found in the rich and educated high caste people and not in the downtrodden outcastes. It must be a reaction to the treatment he receives from the high caste people.

Though he has a number of characteristics of a hero, he cannot revolt openly against exploitation as a modern hero does. He belongs to the transitional period. His father

Lakha symbolizes the servile attitude of the last generation who cannot even think about the revolt. The feeling of revolt grows in Bakha's consciousness due to the bitter experiences he has. However this urge to revolt could never be materialized as it was practically not possible for an outcaste to revolt against the higher classes. This passivity or helplessness of Bakha is a true reflection of social reality in the then India. The only difference that is found between Bakha and his father is that the idea of revolt infused in Bakha's mind can never ever be thought of by his father. There is at least a ray of hope, which is found in Bakha possibly because Bakha happens to be a child of modern India.

The theme of exploitation is best expressed through the character of Sohini, Bakha's sister. She not only exemplifies caste exploitation but also sex exploitation. As a caste-exploited, she is shown waiting patiently for a long time when she goes to fetch water from the caste well. "She had in her docile and peaceful bearing." Gulabo, a washer woman, a caste superior to all other outcastes exploits Sohini. "Now Sohini, being of the low caste among the outcastes would naturally be looked down upon by Gulabo". She not only abuses the sweeper girl but also rushes to hit her. Sohini behaves unlike any other outcaste woman. When other women make servile appeal and show their abject humility to the passerby high caste Hindus to draw the water from the well, she sits patiently away from them.

She becomes the victim of sexual exploitation due to her caste and poverty. She is very beautiful but she has not enough clothes to protect her beauty from the hungry eyes of the male. Saros Cowasjee in So Many Freedoms observes:

Her figure could have viewed with the sculptured images of Konark and Khajuraho, but she has been condemned by birth to walk the path of the outcastes and to suffer their mortification.

When the Pandit tries to molest her, she screams to protest, but when the priest accuses her for polluting him she remains wonderstruck. She realizes that no one will believe her. She stops her brother from taking any aggressive action against the priest and returns home. She accepts her humiliation with the docile humility of the woman of her caste.

Bakha's father Lakha is the symbol of passive submission to the exploitation by the high castes. He represents the force of tradition, orthodoxy and conservation. He does not blame the high caste for the exploitation but blames himself for this fate. He believes that his birth in the low caste is the result of their sins committed by him in the previous birth. He does not get angry even when Bakha tells him about the molestation of his daughter. He cannot even think about revolt against the stubborn order. He is so afraid of them all that when Bakha talks about retaliation, he says, "We cannot do that. They are our superiors. One word of theirs is sufficient against all that we might say before the police. They are our masters. We must respect them and do as they tell us. Some of them are kind."

Bakha's thought of retaliation against the established system becomes significant when we compare it with the passive submission of Lakha to it. Pandit Kali Nath is the priest of the temple in the town. This so- called custodian of Hindu religion and culture turns out an ill-humoured devil. Though he is a priest he lacks the real strength of a spiritual person. His moral weakness is exposed when he tries to seduce a sweeper girl. When he fails in his sexual assault he accuses her for defiling him. Through the character of Kali Nath, Anand brings out the underlying hypocrisy of the high caste advocates of the so called morality and culture. It has been a custom in most of the villages of India to convert the low caste girls into '*Devdasis*'. The girls are married to the god but are used by the priests to satisfy their sex hunger.

Those who firmly believe that the touch of the outcaste defile them, do not get defiled when they sleep with the untouchable women.

Colonel Hutchinson, the chief of the local Salvation Army, and a Christian missionary is a symbol of the Christian assault on the Hindu religion. The Christian missionaries always tried to take advantage of the Hindu superstitions. They were always behind the untouchables because they knew they could be easily victimized. The poor outcastes who were exploited by their own religion could be easily converted into Christianity. Hutchinson represents this colonial exploitation. He always carries a number of copies of Hindustani translation of the Bible and the Gospels and always looks for the possible 'victims'. When he finds Bakha in a miserable condition, he takes him to the church but fails to persuade him to be converted. Anand holds the character of Hutchinson as a caricature of a missionary.

A few characters like Hawaldar Charat Singh, Pandit Kalinath, Colonel Hutchinson do not belong to the low caste society. But all these characters are rooted in reality. They are true to life and convincing. Anand says that his characters are concrete human beings and not generalized symbols. He says that he has tried to create rough characters in all their authenticity. Some of the critics say that his characters are type characters. But Pramod Kumar Singh in Contemporary Indian Novelists says,

Type characters are condition of the socialistic novels... The plot moves in space and characters are fixed to their intended roles or behavior. (Singh 23)

As exploitation is the major theme of *Untouchable,* it

deals with different types of exploitations such as social, economic, political, religious and sexual exploitation. But social exploitation is at the root of all other exploitations. The class discrimination on the basis of birth, which gives some castes undue advantage over other castes, can be called social exploitation.

Untouchable is an inner conflict of an individual who is caught in the web of an age old caste system. P. K. Rajan in his studies in Mulk Raj Anand says,

> It is the individual's quest for freedom in a social system of ruthless exploitation. Bakha as an untouchable seeks his freedom in the feudal society with its unquestionable faith in the infallibility of caste discrimination, with its hypocrisy, cruelty, deceit and inhumanity. We see him stand passive and bewildered at the immensity of horror, hoping for a change.

Anand shows his concern over the organized evil in the society which is the cause of the miseries of the outcaste downtrodden. This organized evil is the real enemy of the society. It deliberately denies the basic human rights to the unprivileged class. Caste system kills the human dignity by giving an unfair advantage to a certain class over the others on the basis of their birth which damages the homogeneity of the society.

Anand wants to awaken the exploited, suppressed, dehumanized classes of the society. He feels that exploiting the proletariat has been our national sin which we have been committing for centuries together. They are forced to such a depth that they will sink lower and lower and cannot rise above. They have been pushed to such a lowly life that it makes them feel subhuman. Anand wants to uplift them from the deeps. Bakha endures his social exploitation for quite a long time in the novel.

The smoldering rage of Bakha is followed by his helplessness and remorse. When Sohini is molested by Pandit Kali Nath, he reacts instinctively.

He felt he could kill them all. He looked ruthless, deadly pale and livid with anger and rage.

But after sometime his sense of fear comes back. He feels weak. He could not overstep the barriers, which conventions of his superiors had built up to protect their weakness against him. Anand wants to highlight that even the untouchables are human beings. Though the patience is the badge of the low caste, there is limit to human endurance. The awareness of this abject humility in the blood of the untouchables does not allow Anand to make his protagonist revolt against the exploitation. He neither revolts nor runs away. He does not try actively to change the circumstances. The protagonist's revolt against the exploitation would have been unrealistic in the Indian social scenario of Pre Independent India. Anand only wants the readers to realize the pangs of an untouchable who for no fault of his own is exploited by the high caste. The verbal and physical abuse and humiliation which he faces creates sympathy for the low caste exploited and anger at the high caste exploiters. He wants the reader to listen to the untouchable's cry.

Bakha's retreat at the temple shows his submission to the tradition and established norms, rather than the defeat of his conscience. He becomes acutely conscious of his social exploitation. This awareness alienates him not only from the higher castes but also from his own caste. The slice of bread thrown by a woman of a big house completes the process of alienation. Bakha's oscillation between rage and despair comes to an end.

With every incident of exploitation by the high caste,

Bakha is alienated from the society. He shows his anguish over humiliation of his friends by asking them to throw the sweets at him. The shame of untouchablility accompanies him like a shadow. When he joins the crowd at Golbagh to listen to Gandhi, he observes everything with the same detachment.

Through Bakha's monologues, Anand puts forth some of the basic questions on the Hindu caste system. It is not only high caste Hindus but the outcaste Hindus who do not belong to the sweepers, treat sweepers as untouchables of lower grade as it is already discussed. They allow the animals like bulls to rush through the streets but do not allow the untouchables to walk through the same streets. Through the scenes of stinking bull he highlights the inhuman treatment given to the untouchables. Anand wants to analyze the predicament of the untouchables and pernicious effect of social discrimination on them through Bakha's reflections. Denial of education to the outcastes is a part of social exploitation. Bakha aspires after education and wishes to go to school when he was a child.

"But then his father had told him that the schools were meant for the *babus*, not for *bhangis*. He hadn't understood the reason for that then."

The reason is, the education would have made them revolt against injustice. The ignorance of the exploited is a bliss for the exploiters. The abject humility among the untouchables is the result of the sense of inferiority complex and docile acceptance of the laws of fate. They do not blame the high caste ones for their exploitation, neither do they hate them.

By confronting supreme arrogance of the high caste exploiters against the low caste exploited, Anand creates sympathy for the low caste. Those who clean dirt are treated like dirt by the high castes.

The caste Hindu feels, "They ought to be wiped off the surface of the Earth!". On the contrary, Anand shows the depression of the untouchables through the question of the protagonist "What have I done to deserve all this?"

The rich Hindus feed the idle priests and sadhus with sumptuous, fresh cooked food but throw a stale and dry thin slice of bread at the outcastes who work for them. A high caste Hindu woman offers fresh meal to a sadhu who does nothing for her but she asks Bakha to clean the drain to get a slice of bread. She asks her son to relieve himself in the drain so that the sweeper will clear it away. "He was too disgusted to clean the drain after this especially, as the little boy sat relieving himself before him". Ironically, these women expect that the untouchables should call them 'mothers' but they treat the untouchables unmotherly, even worse than animals. They are more kind to the animals than to the untouchables. They do not allow them to touch them though they touch even the stinking animals like cows and bulls.

The outcastes are exploited by almost all on economic level too. The sweetmeat-seller manipulates the scales to cheat the outcastes knowing that they will not protest.

The shopkeepers always deceived the sweepers and poor people, charging them much bigger prices, as if to compensate themselves for the pollution they allowed by dealing with the outcastes.

Anand exposes the hypocrisy of these high caste shop keepers even. They accept the money paid by the outcaste by splashing water on it and throw at them the things they buy.

He caught the *jalebis* which the confectioner threw at him like a cricket ball, placed four nickel coins on the shoe-board for confectioner's assistant who stood ready to splash some water on them.

The superiority and the inferiority complex are both deeply rooted in the high caste and the low caste respectively. The high caste Brahmin feels that to praise the low caste is below his prestige. When the low caste praises him, he accepts the praise with reservation. Anand says, "Charat Singh was feeling kind, he did not relax the grin which symbolized two thousand years of racial and caste superiority". On the contrary, a low caste person must accept the generous act with servility inherited from their forefathers. When Bakha is sympathized, "A soft smile lingered on his lips, the smile of a slave overjoyed at the condescension of his master, more akin to pride than to happiness". Ramcharan, a low caste boy feels proud of being even an illegitimate son, of a high caste Hindu father. All this happens due to their ignorance and lack of education. Gulabo takes pride in being a mistress of a high caste Hindu. Lakha advises Bakha to bear the injustice with patience and fortitude in order to reborn into the higher caste.

Anand's presentation of the high caste exploiters and the low caste exploited ones is very objective and balanced. While showing the scathing woman from the big house he does not fail to show a kind woman in the same lane who treats Bakha as a human being. Hawaldar Charat Singh not only allows him to go to his kitchen but also offers him tea from his own cup; on the contrary a low caste woman Gulabo treats Sohini with malice. If Kali Nath is a symbol of hypocrisy and hunger for food and sex, Rakha is a symbol of dirt and filth of untouchables.

Anand has sympathy for the low castes but he does not spare them for their meek submission to the exploiters and condemns their passive abject acceptance of exploitation. He does not fail to show the social discrimination even in the low castes. Many a time people are kind hearted but the rigid system does not allow them to show their kindness. They do not listen to their conscience when Lakha violates the religious bindings and touches Hakim's feet to request him for his son's life. The Hakim gets angry for defiling him by a bhangi but when he realizes the seriousness, he rushes to Lakha's house and saves his child. Sexual exploitation of Bakha's sister is symbolic. The molestation of the untouchables by the high caste landlords, moneylenders and the so called custodians of religion is very common throughout the countryside of India. They look at the low caste women as objects of sexual satisfaction.

When Sohini protests against the sexual assault by Pandit Kali Nath, he abuses her for defiling him. The people, who gather around, know the truth well but the indecent aggression of the priest towards the untouchable girl is tolerated by them because of the superiority of Brahmins in the caste hierarchy. Even the teen-aged Sohini who suffers humiliation understands that the attempt made by the Pandit cannot be retaliated. Even her brother's impotent anger has no value. They have to accept it. However, through the temple incident Anand has succeeded in showing that the outcastes have the potential to hit back. Mere advance of Bakha with clinched fist makes the crowd run away. The same incident shows the cowardliness of the high caste exploiters too. When the Pandit fails in his attempt to molest Sohini he levels the charge of defiling against her and disappears in the crowd. Anand feels that somehow Hindu religion itself is responsible for this social discrimination. He condemns the temples as being the instruments of exploitation. He makes sarcastic remarks on Hindu gods and rituals. He laughs at the multiplicity of Hindu gods. The high castes use their gods for their own advantage. They create fear in the minds of the outcastes. While going to the temple Bakha feels 'The temple seemed to advance towards him like a monster".

Anand expresses his anger, agony and despair of the exploitation of the outcastes in the name of religion.

Through the miserable plight of untouchables he wants to make the reader aware of the horrors of the poverty and sufferings. He makes us sensitive to the heartlessness of a few who thwart the promising life of the helpless young low caste. They exploit the poor in the name of religion. Brahmin priests and Mahants who are the so called custodians of religion enjoy special privileges and positions in the society. They are allowed to summon anyone to work for them. They allow the sweepers to clean the courtyard of the temple but do not allow them even to tread the steps of the temple. They keep themselves away from the shadows of the outcastes but do not hesitate to molest their girls.

Government's negligence of the untouchability is an example of political exploitation. By not making any law against the evil practice of untouchability they allow the superstitions to continue. They know that inhuman treatment given to the untouchables by their own people sow the seeds of revolt against the rigid caste system. They also know the fact that the untouchables can be easily converted into Christians and they succeeded in their mission as one can find in the study of Indian History. In *Untouchable* Anand has made a caricature of the white missionaries. Colonel Hunchinson, a missionary takes advantage of Bakha's miserable condition and tries to attract him towards Christianity. Ironically, Bakha who tries to imitate the sahib's appearance does not find anything attractive in the Christian religion. This is yet another kind of colonial exploitation of the downtrodden. He however does not fall a victim to his psychological exploitation. Bakha's driving the strength from the sun shows his faith in the Hindu religion. But being a Hindu, himself, he is doomed to suffer monstrous injustice. The pompous behaviour of a Christian priest is thus not quite different from that of the Hindu Pandit.

Economic exploitation has been a common cause of poverty and hunger in the countryside of India. This has been the subject of a number of Anand's novels. The landlords and moneylenders exploit the peasants and become the cause of their poverty and hunger. The exploited have no liberty to earn their living. They are at the mercy of the exploiters for their basic needs. The sweepers work for the high castes but they do not get anything in return. They beg for food, water and clothes. The description of the outcaste colony in the beginning of the novel reveals not only poverty but also the subhuman level of their existence. The entire set up where Bakha lives with his family reveals the poverty of the downtrodden.

There lived the scavengers, the leather-workers, the washer men, the barbers, the water carriers, the grass cutters and other out castes from Hindu society. A brook ran near the lane, once with crystal-clear water now soiled by the dirt and fifth of the public latrines situated about it, the odour of the hides and skins of dead carcasses left to dry on its banks, the dung of donkeys, sheep, horses, cows and buffaloes heaped up to be made into fuel cakes. The absence of the drainage system had, through the rains of various seasons, made of the quarter a marsh which gave out the most offensive smell. And altogether the ramparts of human and animal refuse that lay on the outskirts of this little colony, and the ugliness, the squalor and the misery which lay within it, made it an 'uncongenial' place to live in.

The castes which look after the cleanliness of the high castes are destined to live in dirt. Anand holds the mirror to the inhuman practices of the Hindu social structure. Bakha lives in a cave-like, dingy, dark one-room mud house. He sleeps on a faded blue carpet under a worn-out greasy blanket. His father and brother sleep on a broken string bed under a patched quilt. Bakha buys second hand clothes from the rag-seller's shop. Bakha's sister cannot wear bodice under her muslin shirt. They cannot buy high quality sweets; they can afford to buy only low quality sweets like *jalebis*.

The high caste Hindus are responsible for such a poverty stricken plight of the outcastes. Unfortunately nobody in the colony is aware of their subhuman life. Bakha and other untouchables clean latrines but are not allowed to use them. Only the rich high castes are allowed to use latrine. The poor low caste men and women squat in the open outside the city, on account of which the goras call them "*Kala Adami Zamin par hagane wala*".

Bakha's poverty is revealed through the incident of his willingness to buy some sweets. He considers 'Dare I buy some sweets?' After considering all varieties of sweets he decides to buy jalebis. Even the confectioner knows the sweepers taste and limits. "Sweepers should not buy sweets, if at all they buy, it should only be coarse stuff like *jalebis*". When Bakha buys *jalebis*, "He was vaguely ashamed and self conscious at being seen buying sweats". The entire family of Bakha depends on the high caste Hindus for their meals. It seems all have to go through the lanes of the town to beg for food. When Bakha fails to get enough food for their lunch, Rakha, his brother goes and begs.

When Bakha watches the beggars at the railway station, he feels "a sadistic delight staring at the beggars moaning for alms but not receiving any". He finds them despicable. Their moaning, wailings and blessings oppress him. The beggars at the railway station exhibit poverty in general.

The pavements were crowded with beggars. A woman wailed for food outside one of many cook shops which lined one side of the road. She had a little child in her arms, another child in her bag on her back, a third holding on to her skirt. Some boys were running behind the stream of carriages begging for coppers.

He hopes for happiness for the entire outcaste downtrodden who try their level best to exist under exploitation and strive for the better life. He feels that if the poverty is alleviated, they can free themselves from the slavery. One of the solutions to free them from untouchability is to change their professions. By Gandhi's spiritual message, Anand brings Bakha back to his normal senses. Gandhi's words '*Harijan*' and 'cleaners of Hindu religion' replace his humiliation by pride. The discussions which follow the speech make us realize that Gandhi's spirituality, supported by modern technology can give us a genuine solution of using flush system to the problem of untouchability. Anand proposes modernization through industrialization within the ideological framework of Gandhism. Gandhi's speech works as a unifying factor. He looks at Gandhi, "first with a (delete 'a') mixed feelings of wonder, reverence and fear". But later he starts feeling "something intimate and warm about him" (197) Gandhi makes him aware of the fact that "untouchability was not sanctioned by religion."(199) Gandhi makes him aware of their rights saying that they should ask for food grains as their right to labour charges and not contaminated, thrown away food or the 'leavings' from the plates of the high caste.

Some of the critics claim that Anand's *Untouchable*, like his other novels, is a presentation of Marx's philosophy. Instead of Marxist idea of retaliation against the privileged, Anand seems to be more convinced by the Gandhian philosophy of non-violence. He expects a change in the attitude of the exploiters as a result of a nonviolent submission by the exploited. He followed Gandhi closely while writing the novel. He stayed in Sabarmati ashram and corrected the manuscript following the instruction of Gandhi. Thus Anand seems to be influenced by Gandhi and not by Marx. Marx opined that religion was the opiate of mankind and it must be done away in the interest of human welfare. He condemns the priests who stand as middlemen between the God and the worshipper. They create a gap between the god and worshippers and provide opportunities of exploitation. Marx wanted to give a revolutionary gospel to the poor and the downtrodden. On the contrary, Gandhi wanted to remove poverty, which is the cause of exploitation and make them aware of their rights. He wanted them to fight against the exploiters, not with violence but with non-violence. Anand feels that making the outcastes aware of their exploitation by the high castes is the first step towards their emancipation. The identity crisis through which Bakha undergoes and his realization of untouchability thus form the major theme of this novel.

Anand's exploration of the theme of untouchability when Gandhi was raising his voice against it through mass movement is not a sheer coincidence. It shows Anand's faith in Gandhi's ideology and his own concern about untouchability. Gandhi wanted Anand to write in the form of a documentary but Anand preferred the form of fiction. By portraying the happenings in a single day of the life of an untouchable scavenger, he succeeds in driving home the futility in their ideas of caste superiority. Anand's realistic presentation made Untouchable a historical document.

Coolie

Mulk Raj Anand's second novel *Coolie* is written within three months and got it published without much difficulty in 1936, within a year after the publication of *Untouchable*. It was widely praised by the readers and the critics alike. The popularity of the novel can be judged by the fact that the novel has been translated into more than thirty-eight languages. Some call it an 'epic of misery,' others call it an 'odyssey' of a coolie. Anand himself calls it a Whitman poem *A Passage to India*, V.S. Pritchett praises it as a political novel of high order.

Anand calls this novel a Whitman's poem, *A Passage to India* not for its poetic quality but for its picaresque nature.

It moves from hills to the plain, village to city from the north to the west and again to the north. Anand wants to show in all its varied nuances, that exploitation is same everywhere. It is not the religion, race or caste but only cash and class that matter. They all exploit the poor. Munoo, an orphan, naïve hill boy of hardly fourteen is compelled to move from place to place against his will in order to earn his living. His father dies of the feudal exploitation and mother of poverty and hunger. An orphan faces domestic exploitation at the hands of his uncle and aunt. They find their nephew, fourteen year old boy, old enough not only to earn his own living but also to support his uncle who works as a '*chaparasi*' in one of the banks in the town. They send him to work as a servant in a middle class family in a small town. Here he is exploited by the wife of his master. She treats him like an animal and other members of family treat him like a monkey; an instrument of amusement. In one of such entertaining act in the role of a monkey, he bites the daughter of his master. Nathoo Ram, the master considers it as a sexual assault on his daughter and beats him mercilessly. Munoo can no longer bear the cruelty and slips out of the house.

Prabha Dayal, an owner of the pickle factory in a neighbouring town feels a strange affinity for this orphan boy and takes him home as an errand boy. Fortunately, the kind hearted (kindhearted) wife of Prabha gives him love of his mother. But Ganpat, the partner of his master treats all the workers mercilessly. Ganpat, betrays his partner by spending the clients' money extravagantly on drinking and whoring. Prabha gets ruined. The partner's treachery not only ruins him but also breaks him completely. He sells out his factory and repays the loan. Munoo works as a coolie not only to earn his living but also to help his master. But Prabha returns to his native place leaving Munoo alone.

While wandering to get a job, Munoo meets an

elephant driver who takes him to Bombay. Here with the help of Hari, a mill worker, he gets a job and shelter. A child of fourteen is compelled to work for eleven hours a day on meagre wages. Here the head foreman, Jimmie Thomas whom labourers call Chimta Sahib makes his life miserable. He treats the factory workers as animals. Ratan, a co-worker protects Munoo from his exploitation but pays the penalty by losing his job. The workers go on strike to protest. But instead of reinstalling Ratan, the management gives them a notice of reducing their working hours. To divert the attention of the agitators they spread the rumour that the Hindu child has been kidnapped by a Muslim. The workers enraged with the communal frenzy, spread riot all over the city. Munoo gets hurt in it and cannot return home. In the morning, he meets with an accident. A car knocks him down. The owner of the car, Mrs. Mainwaring takes him to Shimla.

Munoo recovers soon and starts working as a domestic servant and a Rickshaw-puller for Mr. Mainwaring. The strenuous work deteriorates his health. The disease turns out to be Tuberculosis. Despite all the possible treatments, one day, he dies on the lap of his friend.

As the central theme of the novel is exploitation, Anand portrays two classes of characters: the exploiter and the exploited. Munoo is the only major character and a number of minor characters are placed around him in every phase of his life. The characters of British origin in Anand's novels can be divided into two categories. In one category, there are owners of the capitalist machinery like cotton mills, tea estates and banks. In the other category, there is the entire British bureaucracy. In *Coolie,* most of the British characters belong to the first category. They are shown as racist. They willfully ostracize the natives. They are paragons of the capitalist exploitation. All the whites support each other in their brutal exploitation of the natives. They do not assimilate with the natives, because they think that they survive only through the brutal and outright exploitation of the ignorant natives. The characters like Thomas, Mr. Little and Mr. White eke out their existence on the exploitation of the natives only. They are the symbols of callousness of capitalists. They are not only unmindful to the problems of the natives but also reticent about them. They look at the Indians as disease-ridden dirty people.

Anand is concerned with the capitalist nature of the white characters who belong to the class of oppressors. Edward Burra, a well-known critic says, The English occur only as minor characters and are described mostly with an inclination to caricature in fact precisely as they must appear to Indian eyes. It would have been false to Anand's purpose to describe them otherwise. Anand shows their role in contaminating the Indian society by supporting the evils of the class system. Anand has been criticized for presenting English characters as caricatures. An English critic . in Yoke of Pity says, "The Cotton Mill episode shows Anand's sustained attempt to write off the European characters." In the group of Indian minor characters Daya Ram, Babu Nathu Ram, Ganpat, Bibi Uttam Kaur and Sir Todar Mal and his wife belong to the class of exploiters in a restricted sense. They are directly or indirectly responsible for the exploitation of the protagonist. Seth Prabha Dayal, Ratan, Mohan, Hari, a union leader Sauda and two women characters Lakshimi and Parbati all belong to the class of the exploited. Though Munoo is the protagonist, he is a flat passive character. He remains diffident and ineffective till the end. As Riemenschneider points out, Munoo is not the common type of hero we expect to find in a novel. In his opposition to society, he is passive while the society is active. Munoo does not build his own life, which on the contrary, is built for him.

Anand has based Munoo's character on his childhood playmates who were working in a pickle factory and who accepted their lot with fatalism peculiar to the Indian downtrodden. Munoo represents all the children subjected to tyrannies of social class system for no fault of their own. He is a symbol of child labour victimized by the exploitative capitalist system. He also symbolizes all those coolies who are victims of industrialization, beaten from pillar to post, as S.A. Khan rightly says,

> He is one among the millions of coolies tested and formulated by myrid (myriad) forces of class distinction exploitation and dehumanization.... the story of Munoo is quintessentially the story of every exploited individual in India and the pattern of his life is intended to show the pitilessness that lies imbedded in the lives of millions of people who are condemned to lead a life of an unending saga of social depredation.

On account of his being a realistic social novelist, Anand does not make his protagonist a rising force or rebel against the capitalist exploitation but makes him a victim of it. Being a child, he is not even aware of the nature of exploitation; so there is no question of freeing himself from or rebelling against the exploitation. In *Untouchable* Anand has shown his protagonist as both a victim of and a rebel against the caste system but in *Coolie* the arch character is only a victim of the class system.

The want of provisions makes him dream of tasty food to eat, beautiful clothes to wear and of costly toys to play with. He remains innocent throughout the short span of his life. A number of social factors push him into the active mode of life. But, as far as Munoo himself is concerned, he is never, body and soul one with reality. Self realization has been the characteristic feature of almost all Anand's heroes. Munoo also asks himself "What am I – Munoo?... I am Munoo Babu Nathuram's servant. He accepts his identity as a servant or a slave in the very beginning of his saga of miseries. This cannot be called self realization because his level of consciousness is found to be quite low.

Munoo is made aware of the cash nexus but he is never after money. He constantly remains under the fear of losing his job. He becomes a victim of the cash nexus. Prabha can be called a different projection of Munoo. Prabha also had been a coolie earlier but out of sheer hard work he becomes an owner of a pickle factory. Munoo also works hard; but too much work in his early childhood leaves him a victim of tuberculosis, with no hopes of recovery in those days. He is made aware of the social discrimination in the early stage of his life. "There must be two types of people in the world: the rich and the poor." The rich are always exploiters and the poor are always exploited.

Munoo is exposed to all sorts of mental and physical torture. He is forced to live even among the slum dwellers in subhuman conditions. He becomes the hopeless victim of exploitation everywhere. Munoo never shows reluctance to work hard. He expects sympathy and love which he does not get even after whole heartedly sacrificing himself to his employers. He lives under the constant fear of his masters in every phase of his life. In the first phase, his uncle and aunt make his life miserable, in the second phase, his master's wife makes his life hell and in the third phase, his master's partner deprives him of the stable life he wishes to lead. In his Bombay phase, a number of exploiting forces make him spiritually die and finally his last master Mrs. Mainwaring's acts of exploitations kill him physically. What Premila Paul says in her *Thematic study of Mulk Raj Anand* is quite right, "His aspirations, passionate longings and potentialities go waste before they could find fulfillment."

Munoo's entire life seems to be a nightmare. Poverty, hunger and exploitation seem to be transmitted to him from his parents. A few like Prabha Dayal's wife lend him a helping hand in his fight for survival and moments of happiness. But others like Nathu Ram's wife Uttam Kaur give him only packs of miseries and sorrow. S. A. Khan says, "The story of Munoo is the story of unending pain relieved only by some imperfect glimpses of happiness". The glimpses of happiness are given only by those who tested the bitterness of indigence. Thus Anand makes his character voice his own consciousness and touches upon the conscience of the reader. Among the Indian characters Daya Ram is the first person responsible for Munoo's miseries. When Munoo's father loses his land, being the younger brother, he indirectly becomes the victim of the feudal exploitation. Later he is brought up by his brother and sister-inlaw. But he forgets it as soon as he gets married. The greed for money compels him to exploit his fourteen year old nephew. He enjoys the monthly wages of his nephew but does not love or sympathizes with him. Babu Nathu Ram is the second character responsible for the miseries of Munoo. He is a typical lower middle class person who has neither self respect nor any voice of his own. Henpecked Nathu Ram backs his wife in her merciless treatment to Munoo. Biwi Uttam Kaur or Biwiji, exploits her servant to show her class superiority. She does not allow Munoo to play with her children. Under the false superiority complex, Biwi Uttam Kaur makes Munoo's life a hell. She is portrayed as a stern, snobbish Hindu orthodox woman bound by the innumerable customs and taboos. Ganpat is another wicked character responsible for Munoo's miserable condition in the third phase of Munoo's life. Right from the beginning, he shows his cruel nature by abusing Munoo as 'Seducer of his daughter'. By often referring to him as 'the goat face', Anand shows his inhuman nature.

Seth Prabha Dayal, one of a few well-wishers of Munoo can be called a possible projection of Munoo in other circumstances. He comes to city from hills as Munoo does and makes his fortune through hard work. He can be called the only Gandhian character in the novel. He does not forget that he had been a coolie in the past. He shows love for his servants. But his excessive humility ruins his career. He gets bankrupt due to his partner's deceitful conduct. But he sells out his property and repays all the debts. Ratan can be called a significant character of the Bombay phase. In spite of his being a wrestler he is a very kind hearted person. Though he works as a coolie he does not lose his self respect. He helps those who are exploited by the society. He falls short of the moral standards set by employers. He dares to raise his hand against the foreman and the moneylenders who exploit the coolies. In Ratan we find Anand's hope for the future. Through his bravery, the seeds of protest are sown in the minds of workers. Through his leadership, he inspires his co-workers.

As Mr. W. P. England belongs to an ordinary family he has not the sense of alienation for the natives of India. Being an honest man, he feels that he should make clean breast of his actual family background and lower education. But like other white characters he has to show colonial superiority through his behaviour. Jimmie Thomas is an Englishman who symbolizes the colonial exploitation. He is a wicked and repulsive character. Through this character Anand has shown that the people like Jimmie Thomas exploit the Indians due to their colonial power but when wrestlers like Ratan challenge them they show their timidity. It is nonetheless, the true nature of English characters. But the wicked Thomas takes revenge upon Ratan by terminating his services in the nick of time. His tyranny brings all the workers and the factory in trouble and resultantly they go on strike due to his exploitation. He exploits the worker not only on the basis of his power as a government agent but also by his own vested coteries of exploitation in the shape of his private ownership of huts and money lending business.

Mrs. Mainwaring is an Anglo-Indian lady who comes in the last phase of Munoo's life. Anand has severely criticized this character. Saros Cowasjee in his *Coolie: An Assessment observes,* ... Anand gets so involved pillorying the Anglo-Indian woman that he loses sight of his hero. He gives some five pages to sketching her background and her somewhat shady present.

Most of Anand's characters are modelled after his acquaintances. This character seems to be an attempt of Anand to express his feelings against women similar to her. Mrs. Mainwaring is a caricature of an Anglo-Indian lady split between two cultures. She suffers from inferiority complex about her origin. She is torn between the fear of sin and fascination for sex. This contradiction turns her nature into a strange perversity. She treats Munoo with utmost care. But Anand gives a hint, by her strange attraction towards Munoo, as a boy, that she exploits Munoo sexually. By showing her past, which was full of her longing for sex and love, Anand makes us suspect that she arouses Munoo's passion. No doubt, the character of Mrs Mainwaring is an authentic portrayal. But as Saros Cowasjee says, "...the novel does not substantiate the whore the author has shown her to be."

Among Indian women characters, Gujri and Biwi Uttam Kour are shown exploiting Munoo. But in later phases some women give him mental and spiritual solace. Parbati takes care of him like his mother. Her sympathetic words link her with Munoo's mother. Hari's wife Lakshimi understands Munoo's torments when she lulls him to sleep with the incantation. "We belong to suffering! We belong to suffering! My love!" Saros Cowasjee finds fitting conclusion of the novel in her incantation, "We belong to suffering! We belong to suffering."

Anand does not want to present merely a gloomy picture of a coolie in the capitalistic society but he wishes to arouse the conscience of humanity against the ruthless exploitation of the downtrodden. Through the tragedy of Munoo he touches upon the sublime areas of human experience. *Coolie* has been criticized by the Indian critics as 'a novel of propaganda.' Paul Varghese calls it a 'blatant propaganda'. S.C. Harrer also calls it 'downright propaganda. In his essay *The Fire and the Offerings* he observes, *Coolie* demonstrates an early tendency in Anand to present life in terms of proletarian experience and a commentary on the experience, and these two aspects are artificially separated at certain points of authorial intrusion or didactic characterization because of the intellectual limitation of the central character". For the Western critics like C.J. George it is all praise and not merely propaganda. It is "only the photographic fidelity of the hard realities of their subhuman existence". Saros Cowasjee also denies the charge on the basis of the author's violation of the rule of authentic solution to the problem. In his *Coolie: An Assessment,* he says, If there is propaganda in the novel, it is as V.C. Pritchett points out, 'digested completely or, at its worst, as Peter Burra comments, it is propagandist only in the sense that any frank statement of such facts bound to appeal for correction.

A well-known critic of Indian Writings in English, K. R. Srinivasa Iyengar says, "If *Untouchable* is microcosm, *Coolie* is macrocosm". *Coolie* presents the victimizing force of Untouchable in a different form. The place of 'caste' is taken by 'class'. Anand explores the stresses and strains generated in the Indian society as the result of the commercial, capitalistic forces from Europe. They brought into existence a new class arrangement in Indian society. In *Untouchable* he deals with the Indian problems but in Coolie he takes into consideration a universal problem. What Premila Paul says in this regard in her *Thematic study of Mulk Raj Anand* is worth noticing. She says, "Anand's earnest interest in the welfare of the suppressed in particular and man in general is admirable. In Untouchable, Anand deals with a gap between the high castes and the untouchables. But in Coolie he deals with the widening gap between the haves and the haves-not. The class conscious society is shown more complex and monstrous than the caste-ridden society. A western critic Edgell Rickword in *Three Views on Coolie* observes, With *Coolie,* Anand's second novel we are plunged into much more complicated world, a world where apparently everyone is free to move about and earn his living at whatever trade or craft he pleases; but which actually imposes an even more rigid discipline than the old. For the untouchable may be chided or kicked, if he offends the laws of caste, but he has his place in the system... That is what Munoo, the central character of the *Coolie* learns in his short life. And in his drifting from job to job, from his native hills to plain, we get the most vivid panorama of life in India today.

The central theme of the novel is the exploitation of a poor boy by the different forces in the society supported by Indian social rigidity. There are two types of exploitations in general – social and economic. In the former the novelist deals with religious, sexual and domestic exploitation and in the latter, he deals with the feudal, capitalistic and industrial exploitation. P.K. Rajan in his comparative study of *Untouchable* and *Coolie* says that the theme of both the novels is the same. He observes,

> It is an individual's quest for freedom in a social system of ruthless exploitation... The society of coolie is one in which chief form of exploitation is capitalist though the feudal exploitation still remains, Munoo, in his quest for freedom, is squeezed dry by the machinery of capitalist exploitation until he meets his tragic end.

Munoo's saga of miseries begins with the feudal exploitation. As an orphan, he faces domestic exploitation at the hands of his aunt and uncle. Then he is exploited by his master's wife. In a pickle factory he faces industrial exploitation. He is compelled to work for eleven hours a day on meagre wages. In the cotton mill he faces, with other workers, the capitalistic and colonial exploitation. He faces religious exploitation in the form of the communal riot at the end of his Bombay phase. The communal riot can be called a form of capitalist exploitation, because the employers engineer the riot in order to suppress the workers' strike. They use the blind faith of the workers as a weapon against themselves. The poor coolies and the wretched destitutes are victimized. In the final stage he faces physical as well as sexual exploitation by his master. The graph of his exploitation goes up with every phase of his life.

Anand has used his protagonist in most of the novels as his spokesperson but in *Coolie* he uses a minor character as his spokesperson. Munoo, being a child of fourteen cannot serve as the writer's mouthpiece. Anand instead uses a union leader Sauda to give way to his views on the plight of the labourers. Anand poses some genuine problems of the poverty- stricken people through him. By presenting the Charter in which the expectations of the workers from the owners of the factory are given, he tries to show the difference between the rules and the realities. The Charter says that the workers are human beings and not machines. They live in and should be saved from the clutches of the moneylenders. But exactly opposite things happen. The foreman of the cotton mills appoints all the labourers on commission. They are offered such huts to live in that they do not have even essential amenities. Almost all the workers of the factory are indebted to their foreman, pathans and grocers. The interest rates are so exuberant that the maximum part of their meagre wages goes to pay the interest. Anand wants to express his anguish and anger towards such capitalist exploitation.

Though there are laws against such exploitation the rulers are always on the side of the exploiters. Anand shows his anger towards the administrators through the incident of Seth Prabha's arrest and the inhuman treatment given to him. The police arrest him without warrant and torture him, so as to make him admit the crime which he has not committed. The brutal treatment breaks the kindhearted person not only physically but also spiritually. Anand describes, "They struck him blow after blow in wild orgy of excitement, his face set his lips stiff and his body towering over the poor man's frame".

Though there is a law against the child-labour, children are openly exploited in the capitalistic society. They are compelled to work under inhuman and unbearable conditions for long hours on paltry wages. What Premila Paul says in this regard is Anand's intention too. She says, "It is a noxious practice almost built in a capitalistic factory framework". Anand wants to lay bare the social evil of child-labour through the tragedy of Munoo. When Anand was asked by Girija Priyadarshani in her interview with Anand in 1988 about the solution on the problem Anand had answered that labour problem can be solved neither in the British capitalistic manner nor by resorting to communism. It can be solved only by democratic socialism to which he calls a socialistic participatory democracy.

Anand knows that the conscience of the readers must be aroused in order to make the change in the society. He wants to appeal to the people to change their outlook on the society. He gives the motto of human life when he says, "If you cannot do a good deed by which people may remember you, you haven't lived". Human tenderness can be the only solution to the problems of the downtrodden.

K. R. Srinivasa Iyengar feels that Anand wants to say that man should cease to take coolie as "a cheap and useful machine, an uncomplaining target for uses and indignities".

By showing the evil effects of money through a number of characters and incidents, he points out that only money cannot solve the problem. Daya Ram forces his nephew to work to avoid his responsibility to look after him. Ganpat swindles the factory money and spends it on gambling and whores and bankrupts his partner. His ingratitude towards the person who gives him shelter shows evil power of money.

Mrs. Mainwaring marries a number of times to settle herself financially but she is never happy. C.D. Narasimnaihah observes, that Anand wants to show that, economic prosperity is not the criterion of happiness for Munoo.

Anand shows their physical exploitation through the description of their daily routine. He writes,

"Thus they worked from day to day in the dark underworld full of intense heat of blazing furnaces... they ran about bare-foot and naked except for loin-cloths... they worked long hours from down to past midnight so mechanically that they never noticed the movements of their own or each other's hands. Only the sweat trickled down their bodies and irritated them into awareness that they were engaged in a strenuous physical occupation".

The life of workers in it looks less miserable when compared to that of the workers in the cotton mill, under the supervision of the white foreman. He appears to be an enlarged copy of Ganpat. He is shown as a symbol of colonial and capitalistic exploitation. The workers' life on almost subhuman level in the huts is worse than the animals'. They are indebted to the foreman, pathans and even the grocers for their daily bread. The fear of losing the job compels them to suffer mutely. Describing their conditions when they receive the notice of the reduction in working hours Anand writes, the coolies of Sir Geroge White factory crept like ghosts through the waste lands of the mills that afternoon. They seemed to have died all of a sudden; that little spark of life which made them more about willingly had died, and left them queer race of men, dried up, shriveled, hollow-chested, hollow cheeked, hollow-eyed. Their wretchedness has passed beyond the confines of suffering and left them careless, resigned. One can easily judge the outcome of the capitalistic exploitation by the plight of Munoo when he leaves for Shimla. When Munoo leaves Bombay he is not only physically but also mentally and spiritually broken. A fifteen year old boy feels defeated like an old man. Anand says,

But really he was mentally and physically broken. And as he thought of the conditions, under which he had lived, of the intensity of the struggle and the futility of the waves of revolt falling upon the hard rock of privilege and possession, as he thought of Ratan and Hari and Lakshami and the riots, he felt sad and bitter and defeated, like an old man.

This shows that Munoo, a boy of fifteen undergoes the suffering of entire life within the span of two years, due to the industrial or capitalistic exploitation. Machine, which represents industrialization, is shown as a discarding force. Machines are compared with monstrous animals and devils – 'many-headed, many armed chuckling machine god.' It is ironical that in *Untouchable* Anand looks at machine as a solution to the problem of caste conflict whereas in Coolie he shows it as the cause of the class conflict. In class conflict, it becomes the tool of exploitation in the hands of the rich. It eventually leads to sharpen the social stratification.

Machines are the ruthless means of exploitation of the poor. Their owners suck the blood of their users. The exploitation in the mills is so ruthless that C.D. Narsimahian calls Munoo's survival as the triumph of the spirit. Narsimahian is quite right because exploitation kills the natural instinct to react, to fight and to claim one's right to live. Even the leader of the workers, a rebellious character, Ratan who fights for the rights of others feels defeated when he loses his job. He wishes, "I would like to die".

For some critics the industrial exploitation in Sir George White Cotton Mill is an extension of economic exploitation practised in the industries in England. It is the exploitation of the workers by the industrialists. But in the Indian context this exploitation is multi dimensional. It is the exploitation of the working class by the ruling class. The root cause of exploitation in the Indian context is poverty and hunger. The tenants of the landlords and the artisans of the small villages become preys of feudal exploitation and industrial exploitation respectively. The starving poor are compelled to desert their native places to earn their livelihood in towns and cities. They live the life of homeless destitutes.

Anand wants to expose all those social villains in the tragedy of Munoo and wants to make an appeal to the Indian society for the just class division of the society. Leo Tagore in his *Social Justice in Anand's Coolie and Achebe's Things Fall Apart* says, the novel seems to be Anand's perspective on the question of social justice in the Indian context as verified in the life and lot of a poor hill boy. Munoo is a microcosmic reality reflecting and signifying the larger reality of the ever-widening gap between the haves and the have not and the mechanisms that operate in our society in favour of the rich and the powerful and positively hostile to the marginalized and the poor.

Poverty is thus the root cause of all the evils in the life

of the protagonist. Poverty makes his father lose his land and makes his mother unable to bring up her son. Both of them die, leaving their child, an orphan. Thus the root cause of the feudal exploitation is poverty. Even Daya Ram, Munoo's uncle, tries to get rid of his nephew due to poverty. Munoo desperately fights for his survival in every phase of his life. The constant fear of poverty and hunger makes him accept various occupations at various places. He continues his weakening struggle for existence with the dreams of bright future. But he always remains abject and drab.

A. S. Desan, in his essay, *Anand's Art of Fiction: A Journey into Existential Humanism* analyses the cause of Munoo's exploitation. He says, Munoo's plight in *Coolie* is a symbol of societal negation of life, love and natural affection. Death versus life is the predominant emotion of the artist in the novel. The reader is given to understand how terrible and tragic the divide between the rich and the poor is. The reiterated emotion is that the poor belong to suffering by virtue of the divide created by the power of money, which Munoo comes to realize as everything on life.

The realistic picture of poverty can be seen in Anand's depiction of the sordid life of the labourers living in the slums of Bombay: The bodies of numberless coolies lay strewn in tattered garbs. Some were curled up in knots, other lay face downwards on folded arms, others were flat on their chests... He had hardly gone three yards when he stumbled on a heap of patched quilt that half enclosed the rotting flesh of a leper. Sick with disgust and pity and stung by fear he capered aside only to be greeted by the hoarse moan of a sheeping beggar, who protected her little child as she lay close to it, resting her head on her elbow and looking out into the dark with tiger's steel glance in her eyes.

Hari represents all those coolies and beggars when he refers to death as 'a release', an escape from the miserable hell of life. C.D. Naramsimhaiah in *The Swan and the Eagle* says that death has ceased to frighten those poor, it is life that is threat and death, a release.

Munoo, a coolie, in his struggle for existence, yells for the sympathy of his masters. Three characters from the rich class – Seth Prabha Dayal, his wife Parbati and Mrs. Mainwaring give him economic and emotional support. Four characters from the downtrodden – Lakshmi, Hari, Ratan and Mohan support him emotionally. A few from the rich class and the poor class show him sympathy but quite a few from both the classes exploit him.

Considering Gandhian influence on the novel we do not find any real Gandhian character in it. We get some glimpses of it in Seth Prabha Dayal. None else is sketched as a symbol of Gandhian philosophy, however, the entire novel can be called Gandhian critique of capitalism or industrialization. Anand reflects Gandhian ideas about industrialization. Gandhi related the issue of imperial economic exploitation of India to the indictment of machinery. It is the reason of man's indifference to man. Gandhi was against the capitalistic civilization due to its inhumanity. Anand's protagonist first gets fascinated by the machine but, later, the factory appears to be the inferno for him. Through the incident of Ratna's termination from the job and the union leaders' appeal to start a strike he tries to expose communist leaders. Rama Jha in her book *Gandhian Thoughts and Indo-Anglian Novelists*, says, "It is in the handling of this situation Anand's upholding of Gandhian values becomes clear."

Anand is criticized for his pessimistic view in the novel. Being a realistic novelist, he makes his protagonist die. His protagonist gets defeated in his struggle against class system. However, a critic, A. V. Krishna Rao, finds optimism in the pervasive pessimism on the death of Munoo. In his *Indo-*

Anglian Novel and the Changing Tradition he says, It is suggested by the death of Munoo, the coolie belongs to suffering and his life is wholly determined by the ruthless forces of the society but beneath his pervasive pessimism, there is an essential undercurrent of optimism, in that protagonist's death poignantly established the rotten state of society and the consciousness of the need for its drastic reform.

If the end of *Coolie* is compared with that of *Untouchable,* it can be interpreted that the survival of the protagonist in Untouchable is in sharp contrast to that of one in *Coolie.* Anand wants to show the comparative destructive power of the two evils and suggests that one can survive the severity of caste but not that of money.

Two Leaves and a Bud

Anand's *Two Leaves and a Bud* is based on a factual report of the racial or imperial exploitation perpetrated by the British rulers in the early period of their regime. The bitterness with which he does it is worth noticing. Mulk Raj Anand in one of his letters to J.F. Brown says "I conceived *Two Leaves and a Bud* as a poem in suffering. I admit that it is the most bitter of my novels, but it is poetic. Were it a literary reportage, it would be hundred times more bitter."

In the preface to the second edition of *Two Leaves and a Bud* Anand recalls;

> What I to say in it was deep in me from the days when I lived for a while near a plantation in Assam and visited Ceylon and saw the inhumanity and barbarism prevalent there with the consequent dehumanization of the colonials involved in the process..... I would say that the descriptions in Two Leaves and a Bud are comparative under estimates. Only the decent Englishmen at home will not easily believe that their representatives in the

> empire could be guilty of such excesses as are familiar to most of the subject races.

The title of the novel is taken from the refrain sung by the coolies while they work on tea plantation.

> I will make a good sheaf
> Plucking, plucking, plucking
> Two leaves and a Bud
> Two leaves and a Bud (*Two Leaves and a Bud* 110).

It is both crisp and suggestive and though the workers find a tilt and swing in it, it throws light on the monotonous routine of the work. They sing it for relaxation, but they uncover their own drabness. "The little hands clipped the leaves more eagerly and more nervously, two leaves and a bud."

The novel is set in one of the tea-estates, a symbol of colonial exploitation in the British Empire situated on Assam hills in the northeast India. The entire drama takes place on the tea- estate. The protagonist Gangu who is from a small village near Amritsar is taken horizontally from Punjab to Assam. He is compelled to leave his native place on account of the loan his brother had taken against their ancestral land and the house, from the money- lender. The tea estate agent Buta takes him to the tea estate by creating an encouraging picture of the future.

On the tea estate De-la-Harve, the doctor visits the house of the planter Charles-Craft Crook. He talks ironically about the British rule in India and expresses his view that the British should allow the Indians to run their own country. Gangu and his family are given a tiny tin hut to live in. They start working under the supervision of Reggie Hunt, the assistant planter, a symbol of evil and lust. Narian, a coolie, describes him rightly, when he says "He is a very Badmash Sahib and he has no consideration for any one's mother or sister. He is openly living with three coolie women!"

After a week while going to the Bazaar, Gangu realizes that they are paid less than what he used to get alone by working on the fields at his village. He censures the white for the exploitation of the poor villagers. Even at the Bazaar the farmers are compelled to sell their produce at cheap rates and buy the essential commodities on high rates. Gangu returns home with high fever. His wife Sajani who represents "the fastidious village women whose whole life had been spent cleaning and washing and cooking and cleaning again," looks after him. But she herself gets infected and dies. The epidemic of malaria spreads.

The families and the British officers gather in the club to talk about the epidemic. Doctor Harve comes with Doctor Chunilal. Hunt insults him for his being a black doctor and orders the bearer to turn him out. He embodies the racial superiority of the White. Other English officers Ralf, Hitchcock and Twitee support him. Barbara, the daughter of the planter gets disturbed with their arrogance and pompous behaviour. Gangu goes to Burra Sahib (Croft) to borrow money for the funeral of his wife. But due to the fear of infection he orders Gangu to leave at once. Though he is the head of the estate he has neither any craft to mitigate the sufferings of the coolies nor any sympathy to understand their problems. Gangu borrows money from the *baniya* and cremates his wife.

Hunt succeeds in keeping the wife of Sardar Niogi, the supervisor, as his mistress. Chambeli, a dark woman, ex- mistress of Hunt, quarrels with the wife of Niogi. He lathi- charges the coolies gathered to watch the show. Hunt arrives on the spot and orders his supervisors to attack the coolies. Supervisors beat the coolies so mercilessly that one among them dies and a number of others get seriously injured. All of the coolies are provoked. Harwe advises them to retaliate. The angry but frightened group of coolies marches towards the office with Gangu as their leader. But Hunt and Crock stop them on their way and compel them to return.

Gangu visits his neighbour Narain to express his wish to return home. Narain makes him realize how impossible it is even to think about it. He convinces Gangu and others that they have to settle there forever. Croft is disturbed with the unrest among the coolies. He sends the message for the arms and ammunition. The arrival of the plane disturbs the agitators. They run helter-skelter to save themselves from the possible air-raid. The doctor comes to help them but realizes that mutiny has been crushed. He decides to leave India.

The coolies settle down. Gangu is fined for the agitation; and he accepts the charge with the docility of the slave. His economic condition worsens with the interest he has to pay to the *Baniya*. The life becomes miserable to him. Hunt tries to seduce Gangu's daughter Leila in the tea garden. She shouts and runs back to her hut. Hunt follows her and calls her out. When the neighbours gather he gets nervous and shoots his revolver in the air. Gangu rushes to the spot and gets killed by Hunt who shoots him point blank. He is charged with the murder of Gangu. The trial takes places before a nine-man-jury out of whom seven are British declare Hunt 'not guilty'.

As the central theme of the novel is colonial exploitation, Anand portrays two types of characters, the rulers and the ruled. In the former group we have British characters while in the latter Indian characters. Most of the rulers are exploited. Most of the planters are cruel hearted businessmen. Most of the characters are life slike but somehow the British persons represented here are not as true to reality as are the Indian. However, not a single character is developed thoroughly. Most of the English characters are shallow and due to the absence of psychological insight into the Indian characters they are also not so convincingly projected. The British characters are always conscious of their power and racial superiority. There is a somewhat uniform behavioural pattern in them throughout India.

The Indian characters, on the contrary suffer meekly due to their inferiority complex and they surrender to the exploitation by their rulers in order to save themselves from hunger. The central character Gangu is a middle-aged person who can be called a symbol of all those coolies in the early stage of the British colonialism who were lured away from their native places. As a victim of the feudal exploitation in the hands of the landlord at his native place, he is brought into the valley of Assam. Here he becomes the victim of the colonial and capitalistic exploitation. Ill-paid and ill-fed, he is compelled to live in unhealthy and unhygienic conditions. Though he knows that the '*Sahukar*' has been the cause of his plight in the village, he has no other alternative but to repeat his mistake.

Like most of the coolies and peasants, Gangu too is superstitious by nature He considers his exploitation as one more reward for the misdeeds of his past life. But when the exploitations of all sorts weigh heavier on his soul his faith shatters. Some of the critics say it is a tragic flaw in the character of Gangu. A peasant who is superstitious suddenly denies the presence of the god. But through the pessimistic words of Gangu, Anand shows how the strong impact of the colonial exploitation crushes the exploited's faith in god. Though Gangu is a central character, Anand does not make him rebellious. He shows courage to lead the march of the labourers but "a tremor of weakness travelled down his spine". His instinct makes him lead the march but his experience makes him surrender to the exploiters. He cries, "Lord, God, deliver me save me from the wrath of my enemies. My children are young and my heart is weeping."

In the end, Gangu dies at the hands of the exploiter without any fault of his own. However, he does not die the death of a hero. He on the contrary dies like one of the millions of coolies who die of poverty, hunger and exploitation. An unexpected, untimely death of the hero creates anguish in the minds of the readers. The trial which follows the murder of the hero creates intense anger against the colonial, capitalist exploiters, which seems to be the very aim of the novelist.

If Gangu embodies the inferiority of the ruled, Reggie Hunt, the assistant planter embodies the racial superiority of the ruler. He flogs the coolies almost regularly. He calls Indians "crawling black men diseased and rotten". He tries to seduce almost every woman on the plantation. His lust for woman turns him a murderer. A few partial British Jury declare him not guilty and free him to help the British for racial and capitalistic exploitation of the Indians.

John de-la-Harve seems to be the spokesperson of the novelist. Though by birth he is a White, he does not show any sign of racial superiority. He cannot tolerate the vileness of the colonial. We do not find in him shrewdness and cunning, which are the normal qualities of the English blood. His sympathy for the coolies is not superficial like that of the others. His awareness of "the dim anxieties and the strange crushed tenderness of the lives of the coolies" makes him rebel against the British exploitation. He shows guts to stand against his own people. He ironically says to his beloved Barbara that the tea they drink is a symbol of Indian exploitation by them. He does not hesitate to speak with his fellow officers with the bantering manner. Some of the critics call it a flat character like other English characters.

He is a stereotype character who embodies the missionary intention of the novelist. When he fails in his protest, he accepts the punishment passively and leaves the tea estate forever.

Charles-Croft Crook, the planter can be called a symbol of capitalistic exploitation. In Indian characters Narain as a leader overshadows Gangu. Though he leads the coolies he knows how futile their revolt against the ruler is.

The themes of Anand's earlier novels *Coolie* and of *Two Leaves and a Bud* are the same. By shifting the act of the colonial exploitation from the cotton mill in Bombay to the tea plantation in Assam, by replacing innocent child Munoo by an experienced middle aged man Gangu, by replacing the foreman of the cotton mill by the assistant planter of the tea- estate, Anand succeeds in making the point that with a slight difference in the quality and the quantity, the colonial and the capitalistic exploitation is more or less the same everywhere in India. In fact the harassment of the coolies on the tea plantation is more gruesome than that of the cotton mills of the big cities. So Anand is more aggressive and bitter while attacking on the dehumanizing effects of colonialism and capitalism in *Two Leaves and a Bud*.

Through both the novels Anand wants to show that the effects of capitalistic exploitation such as the class system have become more dominant than the caste system in the Indian society. The protagonists of both the novels are high caste Kshatriyas by birth, but these births fail to lift them socially or economically in the capitalistic system because both belong to the same class, that of 'the poor'. High caste Hindus respect Sardar Butaram who is by caste a barber. When the high caste people turn penniless, they are compelled to greet and obey their low caste superiors.

T. Vasudeo Reddy in his essay on the comparative study of Anand's first three novels calls this novel *A crusade against social exploitation.* He says,

> *Two Leaves and a Bud* is more or less a veritable chronicle narrating the novelist's crusade against social exploitations and injustice.... the novel as a whole is a faithful record of tragic fate of a poor peasant who is rather callously denied of the fundamental right to minimum happiness, domestic as well as economic at home and in the society.

Exploitation in all its dimensions is thus the major theme of the novel. He faces capitalistic, colonial, racial and physical exploitation in his life. Sexual exploitation of women is also prevalent in the novel. The writer shows that the root cause of the exploitation is poverty and hunger.

Premila Paul in her thematic study of the novel says that this novel portrays, "the yawning hiatus between the haves and the have-nots, the exploiter and the exploited and the rulers and the ruled." The capitalistic exploitation widens the gap between the rich and the poor. This novel is an example of how the capitalistic exploitation kills the life of the poor labourers on one of the tea-plantations in Assam. This novel can be called a proletarian novel as it centers on the predicament of the poor labourers. It can also be called an example of the cancerous effects of the class system and colonial exploitation.

When the coolies are brought on the Tea-estate, they realize that they have houses to live in but the houses resemble tin boxes which are like furnaces in the hot season and cold storages in the winter. They get neither higher wages nor free pieces of land. They become slaves. A number of sardars keep watch on all of the workers when they are at work. A number of watchmen keep watch on them when they are at rest. No worker is allowed to leave the tea-estate without permission. One of the coolies tells Gangu that he has been working on the tea plantation for the last twelve years but he has not been allowed to see his relatives.

But the employers feel that the peasants are far superior as slaves on the plantation. The wages are ten times better than those of the peasants on the fields at their native places. Though the capitalists profit by millions of rupees through the tea plantations they do not look after even the essential amenities for the workers. When Cholera spreads, the doctor says that last year it killed two hundred coolies. When he tells the planter of the tea-estate to look after the water supply the planters are not willing even to spend one or two lakhs on the employees because they are subhuman and do not deserve the benefits of hygiene. It shows the ruthless attitude of the capitalists. Doctor Harwe says,

> I know that thousand of these coolies may be swept off by the parasites in those wells. And I feel conscience shriven. It would be criminal not to do anything about it since I know the water supply is infected. And considers the company earns millions of pounds every year on their labour, it wouldn't be such a terrible loss for it to spend a lakh to save the coolies from perishing through gnats and vests.

This shows that the capitalists are not concerned with the miserable plight of the coolies on the plantation. They are more interested only in their own profits. In one sentence, Harwe shows the true picture of exploitation. He describes the contents of a cup of tea as "The hunger, the sweat and the despair of a million Indians!" The third phase of exploitation is the colonial exploitation. The coolies on the tea plantation look at the white as their '*Mai Baap*' and expect kind attention from them. But through their brutal treatment the white present themselves as frightening monsters. Even the appearance of the White sahib creates panic among them. They create queer tension in the minds of the coolies at the entrance itself so that the coolies go pale with fear. The whites look at the coolies as barbarians from the point of view of intellect and culture. They treat them as subhuman creatures. They call them born liars. The irony however is this that the Whites pretend to be caretakers of the Coolies. Tweetie, an engineer says,

> ...after all, the coolie is favoured here to some extent. We respect his customs and conventions. He is housed and fed. He can keep goats and fowls. His acts are simple, and he is probably not unhappy. He may be oppressed, no one in truth could deny that, I suppose, but he does not feel it as we should.

Hypocrisy of the whites is also revealed through Croft's statement when he condemns the coolies for their illiteracy in cleanliness and hygiene. When the responsibility of providing clean water lies with them, they blame the coolies for their negligence. They say that the whites are "roasting like a steak on a grill" in Indian climate, when they live in the houses built like Natural Historical Museum, and compel the coolies to live in tin huts which generate unbearable heat.

The whites entertain themselves by constructing tennis courts, polo grounds, gardens and clubs but they do not provide the coolies with essential amenities. They live in such lanes, which are so dirty that hookworm breed and thrive in abundance there. This proves how indifferent they are towards the welfare of the ruled. It also shows how they exaggerate their worst instinct and call out the worst in the Indian.

While presenting the conflict between the two races, Anand gives a proper analysis of the arrogance of the Whites and the submissiveness of the Blacks. The Whites keep the coolies at the safe distance for two reasons. They think themselves to be superior to the coolies and they are also afraid of them. They always find flaws in Indian persons. They call them civilized barbarians who need constant flogging to improve them. They are also of the opinion that without the masters like the British they are bound to perish. "Almost all Englishmen in India believed, with varying degrees of individual emphasis, that the Indians could not rule themselves"(32). Anand says that cowardliness is also the reason behind their aloofness. The Whites know that they are less in number and if the coolies revolt against them they cannot even protect themselves. They guard their living places as well as places of entertainment from the animals and the black men. Even the planter Croft considers his life a risky one because he is under the constant threat of the coolies and labour riots. They gather almost instantly in the club whenever there is even a slightest agitation among the coolies. This is very ironic that they send the message to call the departments of the company defence such as the Police, the Military and even the Air Force for arms and ammunition to crush the possible revolt.

These Whites in India however create quite a different image of theirs in the Western countries by pretending that the whites are respected in India for their superior clothes, praised for their knowledge and admired for their personal qualities. The new officers from England come to India with that image in their minds but soon come to know that they can control the Indians only by keeping them constantly under pressure. Hunt represents all the British in India when he says,

> They (the black) would have over run the White race because of their sheer predominance in numbers if they had not been kept in check. They must be taught to become human beings for they were a thousand years behind. And the Whites could only rule them by putting the fear of God into them and by dealing with them severely when they played monkey tricks.

On the contrary, the Indians, the exploited, quite often prepare an easy way for the exploiters by their too servile behaviour. Neither hunger nor exploitation provokes them to rebel against the exploiters because "Abject submission is there almost second nature". This passive submission to the exploitation at the hands of the rulers is condemned by one of the Whites. Dr. Harwe calls the coolies, "docile, gutless, spineless coolies who never raised their voices except on the day of the Holi". This overall submissive psyche, according to Anand, is the reason of their victimization. Their faith in Indian philosophy of Karma and their superstitions make them submissive. They blame their misdeeds in the past life for their present misfortune. They do not realize their strength and hence underestimate themselves before the whites. B.K.Bhattacharya in one of his articles rightly observes. "These half-clad thousands with the strength of a tiger and innocence of a lamb would take decades to understand that they are human".

Through Dr. Harwe's speech Anand expresses his views about the capitalist rule:

> Why do these swarming, under-nourished, bleary, worm eaten millions of India suffer so? Is it because of the festering swamps of the tropics breed disease and that they cannot check the tribulations of destiny? Certainly it seemed to me so; at first that fate had here conspired with the seasons to obliterate everything capriciously. And it seemed an old civilization in decay... Therein lies the necessity of revolution in this country. On the one hand, the vast masses, prisoners of so many chairs, bearing the physical signs of grief of lassitude, even of death and on the other hand, the supercilious rich, wrapped up in their self-assurance and complacency, never one questioning the ideals of glory, and power and wealth.

Physical exploitation seems to be a very common sight on the tea plantation. They punish the so called lazy coolies through the Indian supervisors. When the agitation breaks, Hunt does not hesitate to ride his horse in the thick crowd.

"Strike them" he yelled to the warders, "strike them". And with his lips tight and his head strung into a wooden hardness, he rode his horse into the thick of the crowd, tumbling on the men, women and children who pushed and groveled and ran in utter confusion. The frightened mob screamed and wailed as they scrambled and rushed in frantic dismay, but he rode straight at them, filled with a wild rage to destroy".

Narain shows the cruelty of the estate owners through the stories of the coolies on the tea plantation. They do not hesitate to kill those who try to escape from their prisons. They do not allow the coolies to form their trade unions. Neither do they allow the leaders of the trade union outside to visit the tea estates. They do not allow reporters to enter so that their brutality should not be revealed. When Anand was criticized for exaggerating the colonial exploitation in the Assam tea estates, Saros Cowasjee defended him by stating that most of the facts are based on the report of the Royal Commission of Labour. In fact "...far from exaggerating matters he has minimized the brutalities of the English Planters and the hardships inflicted on the coolies".

Sexual exploitation is portrayed as a very common feature of the tea plantation. Nobody's mother or sister or even wife is safe on the tea estate. The women coolies are compelled to work on the wages less than those of the male coolies. They leave their children in the baskets while going to the tea gardens. When they return they find many of them lying in the dust or a drain or even dead by the wayside. Motherhood seems to be a bane for the women because many children die of malnutrition and lack of proper nourishment. But they keep on giving birth to the babies in order to increase hands to earn their living. The women coolies are compelled to work as rigorously as male coolies. The supervisors do not hesitate to punish women. The picture of a mother who is chased to the work spot even while she is feeding her child shows how inhuman the rulers are even towards the women. The white compel the coolies to hand over their wives and daughters to them for the sake of fun and frolic and many a time to satisfy their sexual passion. The young officers like Hunt are always in search of young girls and women. Narain tells Gangu that Hunt stays with three women who are wives of the coolies. When Hunt comes to the work sight he tries to exhibit his boasting personality on the women. "The coolie women shuffled like hens at the arrival of a much dreaded cock".

Being the masters, they expect that their slaves should offer their wives and daughters to them willingly. Sometimes they bribe the poor husbands by '*bakshish*' to win their wives. If they protest they use their guns to terrorize them. Hunt offers five acres of land to Niyogi for his wife whereas he lashes one of the coolies, for not giving up his wife to him. When they get fed up with them they throw them away in order to set the new ones. In urban areas the British behave like cunning imposters. But in the remote part like the valley of Assam they behave like wild animals. Here they are not afraid of the poor coolies because they know they will not raise their voice against them.

Apart from this multi dimensional exploitation, coolies are also victims of poverty and hunger. The peasants from various parts of the country join the tea estates as coolies in order to save themselves from the poverty and hunger. But both follow them there too like their shadows. Narain comes to the tea estate as victim of the famine. Three of his brothers and two sons die of hunger. Narain and his wife survive by eating the figs and leaves of trees. They escape from death and come to experience the hell even before the death. Gangu also faces the same destiny. When he broods over his poverty he shows his faith in God's honest intentions. He says,

> I have always said it and I say it now again that though the earth is bought and sold and confiscated, God never meant that to happen, for he doesn't like some persons to have a comfortable living and others to suffer from dire poverty. He has created land enough to maintain all men, and yet many die of hunger and most live under a heavy burden of poverty all their lives, as if the earth were made for a few and not for all men.

Deep in his heart, Gangu knows that he has no hope in the tea estates. He not only accepts his destiny but also becomes indifferent to it. "He felt he wanted no gold, no silver but only food and to exist". Though his senses turn numb by the cruel fate, the sense of hunger stays perennially insistent. The meager wages, the penalty to be paid to the office and persistent demand of money from the moneylender frustrate him to such an extent that he says to Narain:

> Yes brother, money is everything. It is the crux of the worldgold. Gold is the living source of man. Every absurdity appears agreeable in a man on whom gold has smiled, even though he looked like a dog and think like a donkey.

This realization makes him upset. He starts looking at the world with a sense of resignation. There seems to be neither improvement nor escape from the sufferings. When a pregnant woman totters to her feet at the time of agitation and dies before his eyes Gangu says, "Happy death,... with a soul which had tired of pinning in its sorrows". This is the fate of not only that woman but also of Gangu and other coolies at the tea plantation.

Thus the novel portrays the miseries of the Indian coolies under poverty, hunger, and the multiple dimensions of exploitation. Tracing Gandhian impact on the novel, there are neither Gandhian characters not Gandhian philosophy directly delivered. But through the conflict between the two groups 'the rulers' and 'the ruled,' Anand shows the Gandhian influence. The conflict is pitched between the exploiter who represent violence and the exploited who represent submissiveness as a part of 'non violence'. Lindsay a critic rightly says that the book helps us to "understand something of the reality of the Gandhian non-resistant movement where the passivity is rigorously alive with the deep warm togetherness of a folk who own a long memory of peaceful co-operative ways".

While talking about the impact of *Coolie* and *Two Leaves and a Bud,* Kamala Das in her review of one of Anand's novels says, The two novels had done this job as neatly as an assassin's knife killing in me the desire to remain safely ensconced in the feudalistic society of my hometown and just as the knife lies abandoned after the deed is done, the books lay forgotten. Only their message flowed in my veins, causing a rage to rise whenever a laborer was flogged by an irate relative or when a pregnant maid servant lay floating in the well where her rich lover had thrown her at dead of night.

If a poetess like Kamala Das reacts with such a rage against the exploiters, one can say that Anand succeeds in his purpose of writing this novel.

The Sword and the Sickle

The novel, *The Sword and the Sickle,* deals with the exploitation of the Indian peasants by the British Colonialist and the Indian landlords. Anand announced the title of the novel as All Men Are Brothers but on the suggestion of George Orwell, he named it The Sword and the Sickle. It is adapted from a stanza by William Blake in 'Poems from a Note-Book, 1773' :

> The sword sung on the barren heath,
> The Sickle in the fruitful field,
> The Sword he sung a song of death,
> But could not make the sickle yield.

The sword is a symbol of force, born to suppress and defeat, whereas the sickle is a symbol of the suppressed, defeated peasants.

As the novel deals with the theme of exploitation, the title is in concord with the theme of the novel.

There are two plots running parallel to each other throughout the novel. On one hand it is a struggle of Lal Singh a revolutionary who fights for the rights of the peasants and on the other it is a love story of Lalu and Maya. The story of Lal Singh as a revolutionary develops through four phases. The first period is the war-period which deals with Lal Singh's participation in the war, his capture by the enemy and his release. The second phase deals with Lalu's return to his native place. The third phase, which forms the major bulk of the story, deals with Lalu's role in the agrarian agitation. The last phase is Lalu's imprisonment, when he starts dreaming about his future with his wife and his son.

Considering the reflection of reality in the novel, it can be observed that the characters and events in this novel are related to the persons alive and the events occurred in early twenties in one of the provinces of India. The major incident is based on Jawaharlal Nehru's *An Autobiography* (1936) which Anand has reviewed such as Kissan's march towards Allahabad to make the politicians aware of the inhuman treatment to the peasants by the landlord and Nehru's approval to visit the place to make an enquiry form the core of the plot. The arrest of Lalu and his comrades and their trial are historically true. The period at the background of the novel is a transition period in the history of India both politically and socially. Anand observes the changing political and social scenario and comments on them.

Regarding the theme of the novel Krishna Nandan Sinha in his book Mulk Raj Anand calls it a novel of social protest. He says, It (it) is, an emphatic document of peasant life caught in the phase of national regeneration. It seeks to achieve its purpose by dramatizing the class struggle and by offering social criticism.

Some of the critics call it "an intimate picture of Indian rural life" and others call it a novel written with burning sincerity." The attempt is sincere but turns out a monotonous doctrinal writing. He succeeds in making his point through the novel but fails to achieve success as a writer. He gives a realistic picture of the Indian peasants after the First World War. They had been the victims of the exploitation by the landlords and money lenders. But during this period their miseries are intensified by the colonial exploitation. Lal Singh's family becomes the victim of the feudal exploitation. Lal Singh loses almost all the members of his family, his ancestral house and his land. His miseries are doubled by the colonial exploitation. He loses his job in the military as a reward of his services to the British army in the World War. Both these exploitations convert him into a revolutionary. He decides to help the victims of the feudal exploitation. He goes to Rajgrah with a mission "to knit the small landholders, the tenants, the evicted tenants and labourers together and to formulate their immediate and local demands". The feudal system which is prevalent in almost every village of India is responsible for the miserable plight of the peasants. The manner in which the leader of the evicted peasants approaches the landlord shows that they are treated like animals by the landlords.

Whereupon the one eyed man gingerly lifted the

curtain and began to crawl towards the place where shoes were discarded, with his outstretched hands joined before him, his forehead rubbing the ground, his black face closed in a silent, shriveled knot of misery above the neat beard, his body dragging on the floor in a way that was both revolting and yet strangely poignant. A host of other pigmy sized black men crowded in behind him, the whites of their eyes glowing in the black hollows and their joined hands lifted towards the company, cracked, horny and repellent, their whole down- at-heel manner an insult to the light.

Anand throws light on the views of the landlords on the poor peasants through the Count's ironic speech. He says,

> ... I am told that whether empires come or empires go, the peasant is a slow person who goes about with a bowed head under a merciless sky and always continues to do so.... And some say that the peasants persist because there are so many of them, that the loss of a couple of lakhs through death makes no difference.

Nasirabad peasants are evicted from their lands for the nonpayment of the revenue to the landlords due to the failure of the season of harvest. As a result of the famine, peasants are unable to feed their families, but they are compelled to pay the revenue by the landlords and their lords. The tenants who had been cultivating the lands for generation are evicted without any notice and handed over to the new tenants. All this is done by the landlords to show their loyalty to the British and to maintain their pompous life style. There is no other authority for redress of the grievances of the tenants. When the Count asks the peasants why they do not go to the police, one of the peasants says, "The police will beat us if we go to them."

The Manager of the Nasirabad estate kills the son of a tenant "A son was ordered to do forced labour and because he refused, the boy was beaten so mercilessly by the Manager that he died". Nobody dares to raise voice against the Manager. Abject poverty and helplessness compel the parents to go to the court not for justice but to save them from the further wrath of the Manager and to appeal to the Manager through the Count not to evict them from their houses. When the peasants get the news of the murder of the tenant's son they show their helplessness. They do not even express their anger. Anand says, But now they only sat up, crouching or kneeling, their hands still joined, their eyes still blank, which their black brows intensified into a rudimentary abjectness, as if they had been reduced to the last limit of degradation, to the primitive state of their ancient ancestors, in whom waves of conquerors had instilled the darkest fears during two thousand years of history. The shadow of the old fortress, and the moldering, half-buried, discoloured ruins of a grave of the time of a later conquest, filled the air with doom, casting an almost tangible weight of oppression.

The description confirms that docility is in their blood. They cannot raise their voice against the exploitation. On the contrary, the arrogance runs in the very blood of the landlords. They consider that exploitation of the tenants is their birth right. The peasants are inspired by Lalu to show their protest.

When the peasants take out the procession of the dead body of the child, with a view to showing their protest, the Manager attacks the procession through his men and bull dogs. He does not hesitate to fire at the rebellions. The Manager kills one of the peasants and compels them to retreat.

When the peasants succeed in the case against them before the White Magistrate, they grow in confidence. The blind peasant Sukhua gives the landlord 'a resounding slap' "The old days have gone... Lecher! If you go teasing other people's wives, I will teach you a lesson". The violence on the part of peasants is like an eruption of a volcano. They show a kind of arrogance through a number of such acts. A Marxist revolutionary Verma Sahib calls it hooliganism. Anand expresses his own views as a common man through one of the revolutionaries. For instance, the student Razwi says,

> I would like to ask you one or two questions Is it only "hooliganism" when the peasants lift their hands? Is it not "hooliganism" when the landlords or the police beat them up?... why not protest against that "hooliganism" a little?.... why is violence unthinkable and undesirable against those who do violence to us? If the English declare that they won India by the sword and by the sword shall they hold it, why can't we say that we shall won India back by the sword and by the sword shall we beep it!

The feudal exploitation is always supported by the colonial exploitation. The police always support the landlords. They arrest Lalu and the evicted peasants for beating a chaparasi of the cooperative bank but they do not arrest the Count who is involved in the same act. They do not take any action against the Manager who kills the peasant boy by brutal treatment and who shoots a peasant with the gun. The Superintendent of Police, Captain Effendi, helps the Manager in his brutal treatment to the tenants. He directly supports the Nawab to face the agitation of the evicted peasants.s

Through a dialogue between Lalu and Gandhi, Anand confronts with the two attitudes towards the colonial and feudal exploitation. Lal Singh says,

> They (peasant) are suffering from poverty, and are weak. They cannot protect themselves against the continual threat of being beaten up. When we were

> intercepted in our march on the outskirt of Nashirabad, I called on them to hit back. That had the proper effect.

While criticizing the colonialists for their tyranny, Anand does not spare the Indians who help them through their so called loyalty to them. Sukhua calls these black employees 'the Black Sahibs' who are worse than 'the White'. They do not have conscience. They work only for money. Anand observes that the railway officials provide safety only to the rich and not to the crude rustic. Even the 'black sahibs' behave arrogantly with the peasant due to the support of the British. A *chaparasi* of the co-operative bank beats a clerk before the Count. He does not pay heed to the Count (the brown sahib) because he is supported by the White Sahibs. Later the same *chaparasi* and the Police beat Lalu mercilessly, before the crowd.

The laws exist only in the books. The British bend them according to the need of the Landlords. The count observes, If the law of the land needed strengthening in certain respects in favour of property owners, it had our ardent support, as it protected us in the enjoyment of our justly acquired possessions and kept those who possessed nothing in their proper places !"

It is always a Hindustani who is at the throat of another Hindustani. Anand proves it through the Gurkha watchman and the bank chaparasi. Both cross their limits while torturing the poor peasants. They show the arrogance of their white masters while interacting with their own people. But through a sub-Inspector Anand shows that these are some, who do it in order to save their jobs. Anand is very sarcastic about the policemen Lalu says "...God who made the peasants poor made them free, while the sarkar who made the peasants policemen, made them slaves" .

The economic policy of the British can be called the

best example of the colonial exploitation.

They had fixed the prices at which the peasants should sell their crops... and the peasants had to sell whether they wanted to or not. But they had not fixed the prices of the produce of the towns which the peasants wanted to buy.

The exploitation of woman is one of the prime concerns of Mulk Raj Anand. Through Maya he throws light on the problem of widows in India. A widow is treated as an ominous person in Hindu religion. She is proscribed by very rigid rules. Being the daughter of the landlord, Maya suffers more restrictions than the common women. Her servants guard her like watchdogs. She is always chaperoned by her mother. Maya revolts against the social norms as she breaks through the shackles of the vicious society and elopes with her lover and marries him. In the society where widows are looked at as 'fair game', remarriage could have been a good solution. It can give her some status and dignify her in the eyes of the society.

Anand expresses his views on women's dignity and pride through the love story between Lalu and Maya. He wants such a country "where women, who were sold to the highest bidder, have became free to choose their own lives..." (103). By making a widow remarry, Anand tries to bestow that dignity in the rigid social system of the Indians. Maya who thinks that it is a sin to meet a man in privacy, boldly asks Lalu "so you thought women only choose their men freely in vilayat."

Anand also comments on the widening gulf between the rich and the poor. The exploitation of the poor by the rich knows no colour or race. Everywhere it was the same. In fact it seemed to him, there were no black or white people, no yellow or brown people, not even French and German, English and Hindustanis and Chinese and Japanese but there were only two races and two religions in the world, the rich and the poor...

Anand wants to show that due to the colonial and capitalistic exploitation the entire world is divided into only two classes 'the rich' and 'the poor'. The rich are becoming richer and the poor, the poorer. The rich do not consider the poor as human beings due to the barriers between them. Anand expects these barriers to be removed. The Count says, "Once we have broken the barriers that subsist between them; there will rise new morality among them, a new sense of right and wrong".

With the help of so many descriptions, Anand throws light on the plight of the poverty stricken peasants. In the death procession, the peasants cannot even walk due to their physical weakness. But the other peasants half walked, half ran, with eager set faces, as if they were escaping from same evil spirit, their bodies naked above the waists, shining like seals with the sweat that poured down their backs. Their bare legs covered with thick black-brown crusts of skin and dust, their voices subdued.

The entire description throws light on the humiliation of the peasants. Their appearance indicates their poverty and hunger. In such a dire poverty the feudal system compels them to follow certain customs.

The one-eyed man came forward, put four nickel anna pieces at count's feet, according to the custom which the landlord of Nasirabad had established for tenants when they came to air their grievances before him.

Anand wants to show the conflict in the minds of the revolutionaries on the advent of Gandhi on the political scene of India. They fail to achieve their purpose through the violent acts. They look at Gandhi as a man of deformity and at his philosophy with indifference but when they fail in their revolutionary acts; the Count suggests that Gandhi should be called upon. One of the revolutionaries says that

Gandhi has bad opinion about communism. He says,

> ... When a man becomes a god he turns his back an ordinary mortals and lives by a compromise with the other gods and colonial imperialism. According to this new god, Gandhi, the communists are evil people, in league with the Devil who meet in desolate cremation grounds and desecrate the dead, spit on idols in temples, abuse the mighty and temple upon all human decency...

Lalu and the Count both make fun of Tiwari and his Gandhian philosophy. Verma Sahib criticizes Gandhi for his oppose to industrialization. He calls him a man with duel policy. The count says, "Don't you see that he is an ingenious Gujarati bania with the shopkeeper's sure instinct for making money". Lalu calls him devil or a man with physical deformity. Due to all these remarks some of the critics feel that Anand shows his anti-Gandhi and pro-Nehru attitude in this novel. However,it is not true. To understand this impression of the critics based on the different views expressed by the revolutionaries, the period in which the story takes place needs to be taken into consideration. The story takes place at the beginning of the Gandhian age. Anand wants to show the attitudes of the revolutionary groups who were under the domination of the Marxist philosophy and were influenced by the Russian revolution in early twenties.

Anand wants to demonstrate how both the groups think ill about one another. The Count thinks that Gandhi should be tried to solve the crisis. He says, "As you know God appeals to the imagination of our peasants and can still be exploited". By making the two ideologies confront with each other, Anand proves superiority of the non-violence over the revolutionaries' philosophy of 'hit-back'. Anand represents Gandhi's philosophy in most of his novels through a number of characters but in this novel Gandhi himself explains the philosophy of non-violence.

Non-violence does not mean submission to the will of the tyrant. Working under the law of our being, it is possible for a single individual to defy the whole might of an unjust Empire and lay the foundation for that Empire's down fall or its regeneration.

Gandhi's philosophy is brought into the small village by a lawyer and Congress leader Tiwari. He warns the Count against his revolutionary activities. He says, "I am afraid your struggle will not develop in this country, Kanwar sahib if you base it on hatred... As Gandhiji says, our struggle must be completely non-violent...". Gandhian impact on Anand, as in all his other social novels, is clearly visible in this novel too. In fact, this is the only novel in which there is an open encounter between Anand's principal character and Gandhi. In *Untouchable* too Gandhi appears, but he delivers only a public speech. In this novel the encounter scene plays a significant role because it converts the revolutionary protagonist into a Gandhian. He accepts purification through the fire of suffering as Gandhi advises him to do. Mahatma Gandhi expresses his opinion on Lal Singh's act that strength does not come from the physical force. It comes from the inner spiritual will.

Anand, in his contemplation on the novel in 1973 says, I have been condemned for writing *The Sword and the Sickle,* I think unfairly, I feel it is... the only kind of third volume to the trilogy. I wanted to state there the rise of consciousness and awareness of the new sense of brotherhood.... The awareness of brotherhood which Lal Singh declares from jail is a reassertion of faith in the struggle to grow and to fight for survival. This revelation comes to him in jail only after he's seen that he had been a political agitator in the pay of (a) big land-lord turned a leader who cases the people for his own glory,"... I was trying to say that leaders who are going to case people for their own ends, to attain power, are... not the leaders who will bring the destiny of human beings into anything like fulfilment.

The careful scrutiny of the novel shows that Anand succeeds in his mission of portraying political developments in India at the beginning of the Gandhi Era. In conclusion of the exegesis it can be inferred that though the novel sincerely depicts the exploitation of the poor peasants by the landlords under the British rule, it does not find approval among Indian critics due to its artistic failure.

The Road The theme of *Untouchable* (1936) recurred twenty five years later in The Road. Though the setting and characters are changed, the theme of exploitation of the low caste by the high caste is the same. Bulandsheher of Uttar Pradesh is replaced by Govardhan of Haryana. Bhakha is replaced by Bhikhu. Pandit Kalinath is replaced by Pandit Suraj Mani. Mala and Rukmani replaced by Sohini of *Untouchable*. When Saros Cowasjee asked him why he wrote this novel since he had covered much the same ground in *Untouchable*, Anand replied; Well it was a kind of shock to me when I went to live in Haryana, twenty miles from Delhi, in the human empire of Jawaharlal Nehru, to find that the outcastes not only in South India, but in the mixed north were still consigned to the limbs of oblivion. There was something tragic coming to me in the fact that the caste Hindus would not touch the stones carried by the untouchables to make the road, because the stones had been touched by the untouchables. I mentioned this to the great Nehru. He did not believe me. He was quite angry at my mentioning this awkward fact. I said I would prove it him by showing it to him in the 'enchanted mirror'.

Anand wants to point out that attainment of independence has not made any significant change in the misfortune of the untouchables. The low caste people turn a little rebellious but the high caste also turn more rigid in their attitude towards them. Anand suggests that it is necessary for the high caste Hindus to get down from the camel of their conservative attitude to achieve prosperity. Dhooli Singh says "No one can enter the little door sitting on a camel".

The Road deals with a single incident in the life of an untouchable in a small village. The incident of constructing the road to facilitate transportation of milk from Govardhan to Gurgaon, a town nearby creates a conflict between the caste Hindus and the low caste untouchables. The construction of the road shortens the distance between two places but widens the gap between the two classes. The novel opens with the conflict between the high caste Hindu boys and Bhikhu the low caste untouchable on the issue of the untouchables going to the temple. The humiliation of his mother infuriates Bhikhu. When a kind hearted man intervenes, the boys run away muttering filthy abuses.

Bhikhu goes to Dhooli Singh's field to his work on the construction. On his way he broods over the conflict and looks around the well for the landlord's daughter Rukmani whom he loves. A seventeen year old beautiful girl is also drawn towards the untouchable but her mother's advice to beware of the low caste warns her to avoid the thoughts of Bhikhu. She says "I am pure the daughter of the landlord".

Thakur Singh criticizes Dhooli Singh for his close relations with the untouchables and warns him that if they get financially self reliant, the arrogant untouchables will one day dominate the high caste Hindus. He condemns Dhooli Singh for defying 'Dharma'. His arrogance of class superiority makes him believe that exploitation of the low caste is his birth right. On the contrary Dhooli Singh who is equal to the Thakur in social status plays a significant role in the emancipation of the untouchable. He tries to make the Thakur aware of the hardships of the untouchables who have neither land nor work.

The Thakur meets Pandit Suraj Mani, the only Priest of the temple to enforce religious sanctions against Dhooli Singh, but changes his mind and requests him to persuade Dhooli Singh. Pandit Suraj Mani, whom Dhooli Singh calls a crafty Brahmin dog, is shrewd enough to exploit the situation. He decides to go to Dhooli Singh to have a compromise with him.

The Thakur's son Sanju expresses his reluctance to Dhooli Singh towards his son Lachman for his close relations with the untouchables. Lachman tries to protect his father's intention but agrees with his friend's opinion on joining them in the battle against the untouchables. The fear of loosing Rukmani, his would be wife does not allow him to quarrel with Sanju.

Sanju and Lachman set the huts of the untouchables on fire. The untouchables understand that it is a punishment for their children's act against the high caste Hindus. When Dhooli Singh comes to know that his son is behind the arson he feels himself guilty for it and offers shelter to the untouchable victims. He offers them food and clothes. The government agent, Diwan inquires into the incident of arson. Lachman admits his guilt and returns to his father. Sanju, another culprit in the act of arson accepts Dhooli Singh's offer to join them in the task of the construction of the road in order to save himself from the punishment. The Pandit also understands the situation and joins Dhooli Singh.

The Thakur, gets frustrated with his son's sin and Pandit's treachery. But his son returns home soon. He feels guilty of joining the untouchables. After the completion of the road, the Thakur invites Bhikhu home. Rukhmani offers him water in a brass cup. Sanju turns violent for polluting the brass cup and kicks the cup out of Bhikhu's hand. Bhikhu is hurt but does not retaliate. Humiliated, he leaves and walks towards the newly constructed road, in the direction of Delhi "where there would be no caste or outcaste...". The conflict ends with the defeat of the untouchable. The failure makes Bhikhu leave his birth place.

Anand is severely criticized for the protagonist's escapisms. C.J. George in his Mulk Raj Anand : *His Art and Concerns* says, Bhiku is portrayed through the novel as a defiant person who faced the realities of life boldly and with determination. Hence his escapist action at the end of the novel is not in conformity with his character.

Bakha of *Untouchable* and Bhikhu of *Coolie* share almost the same aspirations as well as appearance. But Anand fails to do justice to Bhikhu as a protagonist. Some critics call him a shadow of Bakha, some say that he is a caricature of Bakha. Bakha succeeds in reflecting the pangs of the untouchables through his inner conflict. He thinks about the retaliation against his exploitation but does not take any action. Bhikhu, on the contrary is a little more rebellious. He stands firmly against the high caste Hindu boys to protect his honour. Both face the slap incident and both react almost similarly. Both get furious but succumb to the exploitation. When the Thakur's son slaps "Bhikhu stretched out his to full height again till the Landlord's son cowered back".

Bhikhu is thus the authentic voice of the downtrodden, low caste poor. He is both a victim and a rebel. He has almost all the qualities of the hero. Rukmani finds him, "...young body with the pucca- coloured, even face .... finest man among the outcastes gay and good".

At times, he goes against the rigid social system but realizes that there is no escape from the sufferings. Bhikhu belongs to the class of the exploited but he has guts of the class of the exploiter. Simultaneously, he has a common sense and sanity.

He knows that he is being exploited without any fault on his part. He says that one is a leather worker by profession and not by birth. When he is obstructed by the high caste Hindu boys he protests strongly. He feels "why should he suffer this humiliation now... The bard in him, who felt equal to life inside him if not from his status in the world, summoned up a strange foolhardy courage into his limbs...". He is painfully conscious of his exploitation, of his ill treatment by the boys of the high caste. He knows he is physically capable of hitting them back but he socially is not capable to do so."...he remembered that he was a *chamar* untouchable and controlled himself". He only burns with anger whenever any caste Hindu exploits him. Though Bhikhu is the principal character, Dhooli Singh also occupies a place of equal importance. Anand casts him in the mould of a social reformer. He goes against his own family and caste, for the emancipation of the untouchables. He does not hesitate to bend before an untouchable to express his apology for his son's guilt. Such type of gesture is not only uncommon but also revolutionary on the Indian social background. He performs another revolutionary act by offering shelter to the untouchable women in his house. Though he accepts his religion without any doubt, he feels that the religion should not lay down the hurdles in the construction of the road which paves the way to progress, development and modernity.

He is undaunted by the sneering attitude of the high caste exploiters. It does not mean, however, that he is completely free from the superiority sense of the high caste Hindus. When the Thakur threatens him that his closeness to untouchables may induce his daughter to marry an untouchable, Dhooli Singh says "she will not set her affection on the mean". But when his son involves himself in the arson he frees himself from the shackles of orthodoxy and identifies himself with untouchables.

The female characters in the novel are simple, sincere but suffering souls. There is not much difference between the exploitation of the women of high caste and that of the low caste. If we compare Bhikhu's mother Laxmi, Sanju's mother Bhagwanti and Lachman's mother Sapti with each other, they are found not much different in their attitude towards life. All of them are superstitious, religious, stereotype, rustic women. The same is true about the Thakur's daughter Rukmani and Dhooli Singh's daughter Mala. Both of them are exploited through the dowry system. They do not have their own voice. They cannot venture to break the ties that bind them to the Indian traditions. These female characters are thus relegated to the background. There is no need of elaborate characterization in the development of the central theme as the theme does not deal with the exploitation of an individual. It is an exploitation of one class by other. The novel deals with the conflict between the high caste and the low caste Hindus. The high caste Hindus refuse to touch the stones quarried by the untouchables. The irony here is that the villagers are ready to enjoy the yield of the fields tilled by the untouchables but refuse to touch the stones quarried by them. So the real problem is not of polluting the religion. The untouchables are allowed to walk in the streets. Bhikhu and the boys of high caste Hindus have been friends. They play together and work together on the fields. "The earth had kept them together, but the togetherness had now been lost because money wages had come in". Even Bhikhu says to his mother,

> Since money come into the world there has been less and less love". An advent of the wage system for the work disturbs the high caste Hindus. The landlord says "They hope to ingratiate themselves with the sarkar and earn money so that they can buy the status of the twice born.

This economic independence instills courage in the untouchables to stand against the high caste Hindus. Babu, one of the untouchable friends of Bhikhu shows the awareness of their economic independence when he says, "We are field labourers no more, growling on the earth". He shows courage to comment on high caste Dhooli Singh for the arson. He calls him one among the exploiters when Laxmi tells Bhikhu that it is inauspicious to see a Brahmin's face as first thing in the morning. It appears unusual but the statement clearly indicates that they no more call themselves inferior to the Brahmin. Even Bhikhu's illiterate friends are not riddled with the false sense of karma. They do not regard the caste Hindus in anyway superior to them.

The exploitation of women is yet another dominant theme of The Road. Mala and Rukmini become the victims of the dowry system whereas Bhagwanti and Sapti are the victims of the patriarchal system. Bhagwanti though a wife of the Sarpanch of the village, has no voice of her own. Sapti, goes against her husbands wish but only temporarily. Both Bhagwanti and Sapti are superstitious women. Pandit Suraj Mani takes disadvantage of their blind faith. He compels Sapti to desert her husband and compels Bhagwanti to perform special pooja for his own advantage. Laxmi is the victim of the social exploitation. Being a woman of a low caste, she is not allowed to go to the temple. Rukmani and Mala belong to the high caste but they are not even considered as human beings while arranging their marriages. They are offered by their parents in a bargain for the marriages of their sons. Rukmani exposes her anguish over the social system. "O why, O why were the tribes of men so privileged".

The Road is a symbol of progress, a symbol of sympathetic gesture of the low caste downtrodden towards the high caste Hindus, a symbol of friendship offered by the exploited to the exploiters. The completion of the road symbolizes the advent of modernization but the humiliation of Bhikhu displays rigidity of the orthodox caste system. Anand has been criticized by many for the way the novel ends. According to Premila Paul, the end of the novel "...makes Anand's views quite ambigious". According to C.J.George also, Bhikhu's act of heading towards Delhi is confusing. George says, the hero's action hardly has any symbolic significance. Perhaps Bhikhu must have reached the conclusion that even if prosperity and modernity embrace the village, the attitude of the villagers will not change and untouchability is bound to haunt and harass him and therefore, the solution to his problem may be found in his anonymous mingling with multitudes in Delhi.

As a realistic novelist, Anand does not end the novel with the happy union of the two classes. He knows that untouchability is deeply rooted in the Indian psyche. The high caste youth 'Sanju' accepts the compromise to work with untouchables only superficially. He returns to his people and shows his arrogance, which is his true nature. He kicks the brass cup of water from Bhikhu's hand and mourns. "Our whole house will have to be purified". The attitude of all the friends of Sanju clearly shows that the youth of the high caste Hindus is not ready to accept the change.

This rigidity of the high caste youth compels the low caste youth to think about going far away from their birth places. Bhikhu fails to emancipate himself from his caste bonds and decides to desert his own people. His decision to go to a place where he cannot be recognized by his caste is symbolic. It could be realized as an escape of the protagonist from the bondage of the orthodoxy of the village life and an attempt to plunge into the wide arena of the modernity of the city life.

7

Economic Hardship and Emotional Humiliation in Mulk Raj Anand's *Untouchable*

The novel *Untouchable* is a fictional story set in the so-called outcastes colony outside of an unnamed town during the British rule and is based on the life of the most downtrodden, despised and oppressed section of Indian Society, the outcastes. The story is based on a single day in the life of Bakha, an 18 year old *Bhangi,* who is a toilet cleaner and a sweeper boy. This novel shows the realistic picture of society.

Bakha, the central character of this novel, is the representative of all the down-trodden society in Pre-Independence India. He is a universal figure to show the oppression, injustice and humiliation done to the whole community of the outcastes in India. He symbolizes the hardships and humiliation which has been the fate of untouchables like him. He suffers because of his caste. With Bakha, the central character, there are other characters who also suffer because of their lower caste. The paper focuses on the hardships and emotional humiliation undergone by the untouchables.

Aches and Agonies The untouchables lived in mud-walled cottages huddled in a colony and the people who lived there were the scavengers, the leather workers, the washer men, the barbers, the grass- cutters, the sweepers and other outcastes. The conditions which the untouchables are enforced into are really shocking though one can only share their aches and agonies. Their plight is so dire that even for the fulfillment of the basic needs like water and food, they had to depend on the mercy of high- caste Hindus.

This novel is a faithful record and a transcription of the pathetic plight of untouchables who were subjected to immitigable social indignities only because of their lowly birth.

Bakha was the son of Lakha, the *jamadar* of the *sweepers* and had to start his routine work with his father s cascade of abuses:

> "Get up. Ohe, you Bakhya, ohe, son of pig! ...
>
> Are you up? Get up, you illegally begotten ...

and also with his encounter with high caste people who cannot put up with his very sight. But he was hardworking and he never disobeyed his father despite his repugnance for him and his lifestyle.

Bakha worked in the barracks of a British regiment and was caught by the glamour of the white man s life. The British or Tommies as Bakha called them, treated him with respect despite his caste. The simplest way for Bakha to imitate the Tommies was through "fashun" by which he learned the art of wearing trousers, breeches, coat, boots, etc. He was trying to rise above his caste by westernizing, yet he only received insults from his friends about his dress. They chided him for dressing like a sahib and trying to appear to be something he was not.

The Ordeal of Fetching Water from the Community Well Sohini, Bakha's sister had to go to the community well to fetch water for her tired and thirsty brother. She had to wait near the well for a long time putting up with the lustful men. One of the Hindus, Pandit Kali Nath, drew water for her and called her to his house to clean the courtyard and tried to molest her. But when she shouted to protect herself, he cried out "polluted", "polluted". Bakha arrived at the scene only to remain a mute witness, though his first thought was to beat him up. He desperately went home and told his father:

> They think we are mere dirt, because we clean their dirt.

Assaults in the bazaar Bakha had a few annas (coins) and wanted to buy some sweet to eat. He asked the shopkeeper to give him jalebis for four annas. The shopkeeper cheated him and, though Bakha knew it, he could not complain. The confectioner threw the packet like a cricket ball, placed the coins on the shoe-board for his assistant to splash some water on them and Bakha walked away embarrassed. As he was eating the sweet with delight, he touched a man without his consciousness. The touched man abused him, gathered a crowd around him and said that he should have warned him of his approach as:

> Posh, Posh, sweeper coming

Suddenly one child said that he had beaten children. Though Bakha tried to defend that it was a lie, nobody voiced support him.

"To Bakha, every second seemed an endless age of woe and suffering. His whole demeanour was concentrated in humility, and in his heart there was a queer stirring".

The touched man slapped him and disappeared. Bakha lost his humility for a while but self revelation came to him later when he realized that he was an untouchable.

Polluting the Place of Gods The defiant consciousness or the "faint stirrings of rebellion" which had started in Bakha by the slapping incident began to take an articulate form. He entered the temple courtyard to clean it. He became inquisitive to see the hidden mystery in the temple and to know the reason why people came there to worship. He advanced towards the stairs with a determined step but went back to collect the heaps of rubbish. He then strengthened his will and reached the top step and had glimpse of the hidden mystery. But a Brahmin who was standing below shouted "polluted, polluted, polluted". Immediately, the crowd of people in the temple shouted that he had defiled their whole service.

Woeful Living the *Bhangis* had to clean different houses and the owners gave them some bread to eat. This was their means to get their food. Bakha had to remain content with the rottis thrown at him by the high caste Hindus. The bread fell on the ground and he picked it up and wrapped it in a duster with the other bread he had received. Charat Singh, the Hawaldar, gifted Bakha with a hockey stick and when he was playing with the others, a small child got wounded. Bakha picked him up in his arms and took him to the hall of his house to save him. But the child s mother only said:

> You have defiled my house, besides wounding my son.

Though Bakha tried to do something good, he was only abused and insulted.

Reasoning, Rationalization, Demands Deprived of hope

and fed up with humiliations, Bakha had a difficult day and had to leave his house. He then had three options placed in front of him. First, a Christian missionary invited him to join Christianity so that the untouchability based on the caste could be removed. But Bakha did not like the idea of being called a sinner. He also felt that the religion of his father was in no way inferior to Christianity. Here, the author suggests that replacing one faith with another will not solve the problem of untouchability and their sufferings but will only further complicate the matter.

Economic Hardship and Emotional Humiliation in Mulk Raj Anand's *Untouchable* The second option was the idea of sacrifice from Mahatma Gandhi, who came there to preach against the discrimination of the lower caste. Gandhi recounted the story of a Brahmin boy and a sweeper in his ashram. The Brahmin said to the sweeper that to do his work well, he must do it himself and set an example. This action while appearing to be sympathetic and understanding, only undermines the very existence of an untouchable because it assumes that they are incapable of doing such menial work well. Gandhi then criticized the untouchables by saying that they have to cultivate habits of cleanliness, must get rid of their „evil habits such as drinking liquor, gambling, eating deadmeat and also not to accept leftovers from the plates of high caste Hindus. But Bakha feels and says:

> ...but now, now the Mahatma is blaming us. That is not fair.

This suggests that the author s view of Gandhi and his political rhetoric cannot be idealized because it too contains elements of oppression and humiliation.

The third option as a solution to the entire problem was the flush system. Mulk Raj Anand considered that the caste system can only prevail with the job one carried and the easy way to remove it is to upgrade the work environment and bring dignity to each work so that they are economically uplifted and are no more humiliated.

Is Change At Hand? Thus, the novel *Untouchable* is the story of Bakha who was all enthusiastic and had his own set of dreams. His dreams varied from to dress like a Tommie (Englishman) and also to play hockey. However, his limited means and the circumstances forced him to literally beg for food and get humiliated in each turn of the road.

The nature of their work pulled down bhangis to the last of the table of castes. They were not permitted even to take water from a well. The food was given to them by throwing and if they touched anybody by accident, they were punished. The upper class, however, did not find any untouchability when they molest/molested girls or women from untouchable communities. It is a typical day in the life of the Bhangi, mixed with hunger, hope, small pleasures, humiliations and setbacks.

By the character of Sohini, the author tried to picture the lower caste females. She is the passive sufferer of humiliation. It seems that according to the novel, the only way to alleviate untouchability must come from something beyond the untouchables control and understanding. As E. M. Forster suggests:

> His Indian day is over and the next day will be like it, but on the surface of the earth if not in the depths of the sky, a change is at hand.

8

Predicament of Indian Women in the Works of Mulk Raj Anand

Anand feels that woman, whether she rich or poor, is a marginalized being. Bapsi Sidhwa makes an interesting observation, in this context Colonialism humiliated the men and they in turn humiliated the women. So whenever the condition of society is weak or humbled, women suffer the most. It has given men the only vent for their frustrations. And that pattern continues with expectations of subservience from the women. Anand's women are victims of male aggression, are passive sufferers whose Destiny lies in the hands of men; however effeminate they may be. Women in his novels are subalterns who rarely speak. Anand has given them a voice, a past, a name and finally an identity. Anand knew that social taboos against women, as in the case of untouchability, cannot be changed by legislation alone. Here subalternity has been represented in the novel in terms of gender. Gauri is epitome of life-long suffering and neglect with little resistance to the subjugation, male society has burdened upon her. She is the true case of gendered subaltern. The novel brings forth three phases in the development of her character in conflict with circumstances of her life. In the first phase, she is depicted as submissive, meek and resistant like cow. Panchi, her husband, a chauvinist rules over her like a master over a slave. He forces her to submit to his impatience and pettiness without protest. Her duties are to cook, to clean, to please her husband's libidinous desires and to submit herself humbly to his male chauvinism and physical violence. He asserts his male prerogative to beat and 'chastise the wife if she goes wrong' in the name of 'Dharma.' Though he is free to flout all traditional conventions but insists upon their strict observance by Gauri. Beaten by Panchi and insulted and abused by Kesaro, Gauri finds her life in Piplan Kalan a veritable hell. Broken-hearted due to the unexpected callous behaviour of Panchi, Gauri prepares to leave the house and go back to her parents' house, but unfortunately Indian women after marriage is considered an unnecessary burden by her parents.

Out of resentment, her uncle, Amru, bluntly blames Gauri for all the misfortunes after her arrival. Hopless Gauri is left with no option but to work in people's house in order to survive in this cruel and inhuman society. In the middle chapter, Anand, a great humanist, shows how Gauri, a poor subaltern in this man-made world—mercilessly driven out of her house by her husband even in the critical condition of pregnancy and equally callously treated and bartered to a Seth of Hoshiarpur by her mother, develops self-reliance and little confidence to resist and fight against her oppression and subjugation. And during all her trials, she sustains her faith in the Goddess Gauri and in her traditional role as a Hindu wife. She escapes from the Seth and goes to work in Colonel Mahindra's Hospital; she learns modern values and strength to face the grim challenges of life.

If Gauri is helpless and silently submissive at the beginning of the novel and like a subaltern rarely speaks, at the end she emerges victorious. She furiously retorts, "I am not Sita that the earth will open up and swallow me. I shall just go out and be forgotten of him [...]. She waved her head to forget Sita and thought of the road to the town." But the portrait of the suffering Gauri sullenly on her string cot in a dark room, the Gauri kicked and insulted by her mean husband and the Gauri putting up a defense for her husband in front of her friends and relatives may be more attractive to the reader than the defiant Gauri telling her husband, "If you strike me again, I will hit you back" or the eloquent Gauri lecturing to the old potter Rafique Chacha. Anand seems to suggest that in this modern era of existential struggle, man instead of blindly submitting to the old myth, must garner up strength within the soul as Gods are no longer helpful to Gauri and she helplessly takes a road to the town to seek her emancipation from her subalternity. Anand probably intends to suggest that subjugation and subordination of a subalterns leads to humiliation of spirit and suppression of inherent spiritual fire hidden in every living and breathing human being. As soon as fire kindles through suppressed sensitivity, it leads to terrible protest beyond inhibitions of social conventions and religious ideology. Anand, as a thinker, a humanist, a missionary, and a social reformer now and then expressed the humiliation and social institutions. Gauri is an example of deeper reactions and consequences of suppression and injustice on the basic gender. Gauri's trials, Struggle for assertion and identity serve, what Spivak speaks, "to render indeterminate the boundary between the hum Anand the animal and thereby weaken her entitlement under the spirit, if not the letter of the Law." In her essay, "Can the Subaltern Speak?" Spivak shows how liberal academic feminism could silence the figure of the native woman, the "gendered subaltern."

Thus a study of the subaltern concern shown by Anand in his novels reveals that despite all tall claims of social reformation and technological advancement, nothing really changes for the subalterns in our Indian society. Despite our progress to a more developed world things remain the same let the statistical data and sociological survey reveal another side of the problem. The exploitation of the lower caste by the higher caste is a bitter truth of modern society, and newspapers, media, television frequently and sharply focus on the atrocities and inhumanities inflicted upon these poor subalterns. To refer to the latest heart-reading human tragedy of devastation and death caused by Asian Killer Tsunami tidal waves where death toll went up in millions, and which has made the people of countries across the world reach out and do their bit to help the afflicted humanity, in the relief camps of Nagapattinam caste barriers are forcing Dalits out of the circle of sympathy and relief. Not only have Dalits been thrown out of these camps, but they are not being allowed to collect food and water supplies or use the toilets—simply because they are subalterns—from the Meenavar (fishermen) community that is graded as the most backward class in the social structure. To quote from the Edit page of the Hindustan Times. "But in this horrendous case of entrenched apartheid; ordinary people are to blame for perpetuating a crime in the name of tradition. In Nagapattinam alone, 32 families have not only been told to fend for themselves but have also been shoed away from using basic amenities lest they contaminate "caste Hindus." And this is the aftermath of a tragedy where they, the high ups, themselves have just about survived. Such forced divisions and caste barriers are not sociological necessities but social evils that need to be dismantled, if need be by force.

When one looked at the lot of the less privileged populations, for Instance in a country like India, One noticed how they had been deliberately kept at a level of sub humanity. To Take up the cudgels on behalf of the deprived, Anand has chosen the medium of English, which, he avers, is not really an alien language, and with all our past of exposure to the British rule we are quite at home with English as a medium for an expression of our urges. Only, Anand strongly believes with Raja Rao that "We cannot write like the English. We should not. We can write only as Indians." Thus, the choice of a foreign medium—English—for creative expression does not make Mulk Raj Anand any less Indian in thought and spirit than one would expect a man so deeply immersed in eradicating the social evils that came to prevail in man." G.S. Balarama Gupta rightly observes, for Anand is a humanist all the way and his prime concern is the human predicament in all its dimensions. As a novelist Anand displays an unflagging interest in restoring the basic human rights to the underprivileged and the dispossessed in the Indian society. An exposure of the economic exploitation of the deprived and a castigation of the existing caste and class distinctions in India has been a major preoccupation of the writer.

Recent detractors of Anand like Meenakshi Mukherjee bring him to account for certain experimental aspects of language like the literal translation of Hindi words into English sentences and the changing of the spelling of English words to suggest uneducated speech but a consideration of these lapses can willingly be relegated to the background if one is able to commitment to the extirpation of unjust social discrimination in the community of men. Anand persistently focuses on the trials and tribulations of the "have-notes" and seeks to diminish their anguish. No social injustice ever escapes Anand's observant eye. Religion and social distinctions, he believes, often become reactionary forces, instruments of oppression and obstacles to the development of independent thought. It is in this connection that K.R.S. Iyengar refers to Mulk Raj Anand as one of the few novelists who have shown "anything like stamina and stern consistency of purpose."

The India of the "thirties" was characterized by a national upsurge that Had stirred the entire country on an unprecedented scale and Mulk Raj Anand was a major contributor in bringing about this consciousness among the people of the times. M.K. Naik has aptly referred to him as "the novelist of the social man" for his novels compled the contemporary society into self-awareness and introspection and introspection and aroused the consciences of humanity.

Anand retrieved the Indo-Anglian novel from the domains of history and romance and writing prolifically, led it to take cognizance of the prevailing conditions and the hard realities of the pre-Independence social scene. His first three novels, namely, *Untouchable* (1935), *Coolie* (1936) and *Two Leaves and a Bud* (1937) from a natural trilogy for all three have a victimized, oppressed and outcast protagonist whose lot represents the fate of India enslaved by the British and the lot of the hapless workers indentured to the capitalist system. In these novels, Anand, determined to demolish the rose-tinted edifice of India that prevailed and offered a realistic picture of the country as she actually is, seen in Marxism terms as "a cockpit of the class-struggle and a sordid one at that." India to Anand meant repressive privations, the millstone of the caste-system round the neck of the poorest, adherence to outmoded mores and customs and ceaseless subjection to foreign rule.

Untouchable and *Coolie* are both eye-openers with regard to the maltreatment of the depressed classes in the 1930s. In *Untouchable,* Bakha, a toilet-cleaner, is depicted as a great admirer of the British, wearing clothes cast-off by them and enjoying life to the full, totally oblivious of the "class-feeling" that prevailed among men. It is only when, at the age of eighteen, he happens to touch a Brahmin and the latter flinches from the contact in anger and hatred that he is made aware of his status in the society as "unclean" because of the nature of his work. From then onwards Bakha is conscious of the curse of the untouchable that he has inherited from his father. It is this awakening to painful knowledge that is depicted with great sensitivity by Anand. A temple priest's attempt at molesting Bakha's sister, Sohini, is an alarming exposure of the hypocrisy of the Brahmins who clearly lived in double standards.

The priest who avoided even the shadow of an

absolutely no qualms of conscience. Anand offers three solutions to Bakha to step out of the agony of self-Abasement and ceaseless frustration. A Salvation Army colonel offers conversion to Christianity as a resolution of the problem but without much success. Later, Bakha is drawn to Mahatma Gandhi, Who inspires as well as distresses him when he refers to the Untouchable as God's own people—- the '*Harijans*.' A third solution, Which Anand is inclined to unhderline as the final one, is the one offered by the poet, Iqbal, in the scientific materialistic progress which may, he believes, bring social justice and relief to Bakha and the like. Resolutions to deep- seated problems are, however, not so easy to come by. Anand's commitment to the philosophy of humanism informs every Line of his creative ventures. *Untouchable*, a sensitive record of the events Of (of) a single day in the life of a teenaged sweeper in a small town in the Punjab is neatly assessed by Edgel Rickword as "essentially a tragic poem Of the individual caught in the net of the age-old caste-system," the caste Stratification being an unfortunate characteristic of the decadent Indian Society of the times.

Coolie, the novel that established Anand as a novelist depicting the social realism of the 1930s, does not concentrate on caste consciousness as does *Untouchable*. Picaresque in nature, it is the story of Munoo, the landless peasant, the young innocent boy of fourteen who is compelled to Leave his home in the idyllic hills of North-West India in the late 1920s in search of a livelihood in the plains, a livelihood that would enable him to sustain him amidst all hardships.

Munoo becomes, by turns, a servant, a laborer and a rickshaw puller,(.) Each phase of his life bringing more humiliation than the previous one. The young lad subjected to the corruption rampant in the society and to the pressures of an egocentric world is razed to the ground never to rise again. This effectively demonstrates the helplessness and powerlessness of an underdog in the face of the grinding machinery of economic and religious oppression. Anand's protagonist in this novel was modeled on his own childhood playmate, Munoo, who was consigned to endless labor in a pickle-factory and who accepted his lot in life with total resignation.

Munoo is treated as "the scum of the earth" and is called so when he happens to be standing in front of a Sikh's shop. He is looked upon as a Leper whose very touch would defile others. Added to this are the deprecations heaped on him by the cart-driver. *Coolie* is a saga of unrelieved pain and suffering with glimpses of hope so evanescent that one almost fails to register them. It depicts the travails and tribulations of a wretched and forlorn coolie in a classconscious society where the awareness of this so-called superiority of some in terms of class—economic, cultural and political—has a largely deleterious effect on social cohesion. The sanctity of human relationships is flagrantly violated. The only irrefutable truth that emerges from the mayhem of divisiveness is the ever widening gulf between the rich and the poor, the latter gradually sliding into perpetual misery and ultimate obliteration. Munoo's take can conveniently be divided into three phases. In the first he is an awkward and gauche servant in an Indian household of social climbers who have no reservation in prostrating before the British but whose efforts at rising in social esteem are foiled by the clumsy and inept behaviour of Munoo. Anand's object of satire, here, is the British 'sahib' who is blissfully ignorant of India and the ways of Indians.

In the second phase of his life, Munoo visits a Punjabi town called Daulatpur to work in a pickle-factory there. His lovable nature endears him to the factory owner, Prabha, and his wife, Parbati. Prabha's generosity, however, soon leads him into financial straits and subjects him to violence at the hands of corrupt policemen. Anand's purpose in this series of incidents in the novel is to expose the treachery of men in various capacities—employers, exploiters, policemen and financier. Munoo next goes to Bombay where Anand demonstrates the prevalence of a different kind of capitalism from that of the Daulatpur pickle-factory. Working in a cotton mill owned by a Britisher, Munoo experiences a total loss of identity for he is only one of the herds callously driven to the wall. In his depiction of the harsh life of the workers Anand unmistakably feels strongly and sympathetically for this class. Besides this display of affiliations, his introduction of the communal riots is meant to underscore the communication that capitalists and British imperialists both use communal differences to divide and rule.

In the last phase of his life, Munoo finds himself in an extremely ironic situation. He is taken under the patronage of Mrs. Mainwaring, a rich Eurasian woman in Simla. The mixed traits characterizing Mrs. Mainwaring are neurosis, the maternal instinct and nymphomania. The now handsome and young Munoo becomes the lady's rickshaw puller and lover. This apparently comfortable existence becomes for Munoo his cross for it leads to his ultimate depravity and finally, his inevitable end through the consumption that he has contracted. Before he dies, he listens to the outbursts of his friend, Mohan the communist, who holds the capitalist system responsible for Munoo's fate. It is through Mohan that the writer wishes to declare the "thesis" of his novel which focuses on the evils of a devouring socio-economic system. Munoo, however, has been a victim not only of systems and conventions but of human selfishness and religious fanaticism as well. On the aesthetic and knowledge is a triumph of compiling psychological portrayal. *Two Leaves and a Bud* (1973) the third of the supposed trio of Anand's novels referred to at the very outset is an imaginative account of British oppression in a tea-plantation in Assam. This is another of Anand's novels of indignation and protest in which he dissects and analyzes human motives from an ironical slant. Gangu, the coolie, (an older and maturer version of

Munoo in *Coolie*) is ensnared to join work in a tea-estate in Assam owned by the British. The novel, on the pattern of *Untouchable* and *Coolie*, is, again, a tale of woe—a tale of Gangu's ever-increasing exploitation coming to a grinding halt with his murder by an English overseer, believably, on the verge of insanity. Anand's purpose is again the Indictment of the systems of capitalism and imperialism for their total demolition of the identity of the poor Indian who is vulnerable to assault and Exploitation either by the more privileged Indians or by the insular British who isolate themselves from the Indians but never loses an opportunity to seduce their wives and daughters.

Two Leaves and a Bud, has unmistakable echoes of Fortier's *A passage to India*. The callous and unfeeling British represented by Croft-Cooke, the manager, and Reggie Hunt, a drunkard and a womanizer, are in flagrant disagreement with the humanist. Dr. De La Havre and his beloved, Barbara, both of whom are clearly for the Indians and condemn the latter's exploitation (exploitation) by the British imperialists and capitalists. Anand's irony, however, is not as trenchant at that of Forster for it is diluted to some extent by the tender moving pathos of depiction.

Two Leaves and a Bud dramatizes, like *Untouchable* and *Coolie*, moral issues by the counterpointing of good and evil. Gangu, the protagonist, accompanied by his wife, Sajani, his daughter, Leila, and his son, Budhoo, moves from his native village in the Punjab to distant Assam to take up a job in Macpherson Tea Estate owned by an Englishman. Initially excited at the prospect of starting life afresh in the plantation, Gangu soon comes to realize that his days at the tea estate have been nothing but a series of deprivations—his wife dies, there is an attempt at raping his daughter, Leila, and ultimately, he himself is shot dead by Reggie Hunt. The final moment of disillusionment comes with impact of the communication that Hunt is exonerated of the charge of murder by a British jury.

Much as the novel moves us to compassion and anger, there is no gainsaying the fact that had Anand's "purpose" not intruded so vehemently and persistently upon the aesthetic and imaginative aspect of this work of Fiction, *Two Leaves and a Bud* would have been a novel with a far greater psychological subtlety and a more piercing irony. *Untouchable* and *Coolie* Tend to offer a cogent balance of Anand's propagandist protest and his persuasive sympathetic realism and are relatively more convincing as literary exercises. However, one can, perhaps, relax the stricture against *Two Leaves and a Bud* by suggesting that the novel is intended to be "more an extended moral allegory than an exercise in creating believable human beings."

Mulk Raj Anand was the most important writer that activated the new Wave of realism in the nineteen twenties and the nineteen thirties. All Anand's novels, especially the early—and the misery of the lower castes and classes of India. The novel, a form befitting the aspirations and objectives of a social realist like Anand, remains today—and largely owing to his generous contribution- —the dominant genre for Indo-Anglian writers.

Mulk Raj Anand was an Indian English novelist who depicted the lives of the poor and the downtrodden in his novels. He is the one of the three pillars of Indian writings in English, Raja Rao and R.K. Narayan being the other two. These writers, through their writings, tried to bring respectability and identity to Indian English Literature. These writers made a sincere attempt to articulate the subdued feelings and suppressed emotions of their countrymen. Indian literature was identified as a literature of fairy-tales and fantasy stories in the world. Bengali novelists like Sharat Chandra and Rabindranath Tagore made an Endeavour to bring in a note of realism in their works. The trend was continued by the trio. The Novelists now gathered courage to voice the sufferings of the people under British rule and also under the pressure of out dated customs and oppressive traditions. The society had been reeling under the yoke of slavery for the past hundreds of year. Age old practices of discrimination on the basic of caste and class continued to separate man from man. The society suffered at different levels and at all levels but could not think of uniting regardless of any bias, under one banner of humanity. They remained disintegrated under different flags.

Mulk Raj Anand arrived on the literary scene at such a time. To a sensitive heart like his, this discrimination was digging at the roots and was eating away the vitality of the country. He could see that discrimination rampant in society was weakening the nation. The country could never think of freedom and progress if it continued this evil practice. An effective weapon was in his hands and he left no chance of ameliorating the lot of his countrymen through this weapon. Art to Mulk Raj was not only for the sake of art only; it was for the life and the people. He addressed the problems of caste- system, poverty, squalor, backwardness, ignorance and superstition in his works.

Through his novels he documented the abuses of the exploited class. The importance of a writer lay in his sensitivity towards the human beings. Anand once said,

> [...] What is writer of he is not the fiery voice of the people, who, through his own torments, urges exaltations, by realizing the pains, frustrations, aspirations of others, and by cultivating his incipient powers of expression, transmutes in art all feeling, all thought, all experience—thus becoming the seer of a new vision in any given situation.

Anand's certainly is the fiery voice of the people belonging to the poor class and the untouchables. The trauma of the untouchables has been artistically depicted in Tagore's Chandalika. But Anand's novels has a descriptive quality and has been able to draw the attention of the readers to their pathetic condition. He has successfully communicated the hopes, aspirations, pains and frustrations of this class of society. Anand used his writing talent for the people. He wrote, 'of the people, for the people and as a man of the people.'

Art for him was to ameliorate life and not just for the sake of art. In his realistic treatment of themes, he may be compared with the masters of realism: Balzac and Zola. Through his realistic portrayal of characters and true and bold depiction of the problems of Indian society he hinted to the west that Indian writings have substance, they are not only the stories of fantasy land and fairies only. Looking into the life of Anand we find that he had the first hand experience of the lives of the poor and the lower class of society. His father was a Subedar in Indian Army and he spent a considerable time in the company of the children of servants and sweepers. These very children hailing from unprivileged and deprived class of society, later on, became life-like characters in his novels.

All these heroes, as the other men and women who had emerged in my novels and short stories were dear to me, because they were reflection of the real people, I had known during my childhood and youth [...]. They were not mere phantoms [...]. They were flesh of my flesh and blood of my blood. Anand enjoys the reputation of being a pioneer due to his realism and social Protest. His humanism can be seen in his love for the working class people and the downtrodden.

His protagonists are sweepers, coolies and plantation workers etc. He can be compared with Maxim Gorky because he had the ability to see human qualities in the downtrodden people of society. Each novel is devoted to the problem of one deprived class of society. Untouchablehas (*Untouchable* has) been written from the point of the sweeper who receives sub-human treatment at the hands of upper-caste Hindus.

They treat him like dirt since he cleans dirt since he cleans dirt. *Coolie* deals with the problem of poverty. Munoo, the protagonist says that, there must be only two kinds of people in the world—the rich and the poor.

Two leaves and a Bud, deals with the lives of plantation workers who, even when they worked pretty hard, remained on the verge of starvation. Anand comments on the treatment of imperial administration to the peasants. The poor condition of peasants reeling under debt and poverty has been well delineated in his novels.

Anand has dealt frankly with different kinds of exploitation that Indians faced in the early decades of the century. The Brahmins enjoyed privileges and positions in society. Sudras, the Untouchables (untouchables) faced many kinds of indignities. Another kind of exploitation was that of the Hindu wife. She has been shown as quite helpless against the till treatment meted out to her at the hands of her husband and in-laws. Besides, English people also exploited Indians. Anand says, "The strange color of their skins made them more remote giving them aura of being of another world, frightening in their potencies. And the inhuman steel frame of officialdom which they made them more like the tyrannical demons of hell."

At the same time there was no effort on the part of the English people to reform the outdated religious practices purposely. In the name of giving freedom to Indians, in the observance of their religious practices, they allowed superstitions, and utter ignorance of Indians life. Mulk Raj Anand played an important role in focusing upon these problems.

Anand's literary career was launched by a family tragedy which occurred owing to the rigidity of caste system. His aunt had committed suicide because she was excommunicated by her family for having shared a meal with a Muslim. This incident drew the attention of Anand towards caste system. He saw its worst from in the name of untouchable. The theme has been well elaborated in this novel.

Anand has vividly described the mental anguish of Bakha, the chief protagonist of the novel *Untouchable*. The novel centers on the life of a sweeper boy Bakha. Anand adored this boy as a hero since his childhood, "because he was physically like a God, played all the games superbly and could recite all cantos from the epic poem Heer Ranjha of Waris Shah." He was obsessed with his tragedy which lay in the fact that this extraordinarily talented boy was always insulted by most of the people due to his low caste. He could not get admission in a school as he would defile his classmates by his touch. This novel highlights the social wrongs and injustices meted out to this deprived and dispossessed class of society. Bulashah is a small village in Punjab and there is a small colony named as outcaste's colony. There are, 'a group of mud-walled houses, that clustered together in two rooms under the shadow both of the town and the cantonment, but outside their boundaries and separate from them, their lived the washer men, the barbers, the water-carriers, the grass- cutters and other outcastes of Hindu society.'

Bakha is a young boy of eighteen who has not surrendered to his fate like his father Lakha. He is a child of twentieth century and is given to modern way of dressing. "From a Tommy he has secured a pair of old breeches and from a sepoy a pair of old boots; he would, if he could, like to look like the white foreigner and so be in the 'fasshun.' " He dreams of a good life but as soon as morning dawns his job of toilette-cleaning starts. Three rows of toilettes to be cleaned and that too single-handedly. He has to repeat this process several times in a day. Maintenance of cleanliness is the challenging job he has been allotted and he performs it efficiently. Though the society does not treat him as a human being, he proves to be more human than the so-called protectors of humanity. When a boy gets injured in a hockey game Bakha saves the boy and brings him to his house. Instead of receiving appreciation for this humanitarian act, Bakha receiving appreciation for this humanitarian act, Bakha receives assault and insult because he had polluted the injured by his touch. The height of insult that the members of this community have to face can be judged by the following comment:

> Dirty dog! Son of a bitch! Offspring of a pig! I'll have to go and get washed!

I was going to business and now—now, on account of you I'll be late. These are the comments that Bakha has to listen quite often. He has to listen and continue to clean the road and the toilets: his fate is inescapable. The height of social alienation of this class can be understood by the fact that these people have to announce their arrival whenever they appear in thoroughfares. Another dichotomy is hinted by Anand when he relates the story of Bakha's young and beautiful sister Sohini.. When Sohini goes to the village well to fetch water she waits for some time and then Kali Charan, The priest of the village takes pity on her and fills her pitcher. While filling the pitcher he invites the girl to his house for cleaning the courtyard. Kali Charan kept an evil eye on this girl and wanted an opportunity to molest her. When the girl goes to clean the courtyard he sexually assaults her. Sohini tries to save her honor by crying. A crowed of high-caste people gathered and Kali Charan cried, 'polluted, polluted,' thereby accusing the poor girl of defiling him by her touch. The evildoer and the innocent Sohini is taken to be corrupt by the hypocritical society. The hero of the novel suffers morally, socially and financially. The society treats a sweeper only as a sweeper sans any human feelings and emotions. Bakha is badly frustrated by the caste-prejudices and tries to find the solution from a third party as he gets none from his family or from the society he lives in. Anand gives touching examples to focus on the pitiable condition of this sweeper boy who is not alone in suffering but with him suffers the whole class which he represents.

Coolie deals with the economic exploitation of one man by another, i.e. of the lower class by the upper class. Since India got independence, the wealth and power concentrated in a few hands. The microscopic minority consisting of a few called capitalists dictated the terms to the majority consisting of the poor and the deprived. In order to keep body and soul together, the poor had to work under their masters: the rich, who subjected them to exploitation and persecution. *Coolie* portrays the tribulations of coolies in a class-ridden society. Indian Displayed the same temper as that of British officers. Indian officers too acquired a lot of wealth. Munoo, the protagonist, though is *kshatriya* by caste, but he is poor and he feels that "poverty itself is a caste. The maltreatment reaches such a frightening level that 'life is a threat, and death is release.' Munoo, the protagonist, suffers from the beginning.

His life is a saga of pain and suffering.

First he is tortured by his aunt and uncle as he was an orphan. They send him to the house of an officer to serve them as a domestic servant. He receives sub-human treatment there also. He changes the job and joins a pickle factory and later on serves as a coolie in the Bazar of Daulatpur. His search for a better living brings him to Bombay where he serves as a laborer in a cotton mill. He gets injured in a class between the capitalists and laborers. Getting hurt, he is pitied upon by a European lady and acts as her rickshaw-puller. Unable to bear the burden and strain of this job, he meets his tragic end. The entire novel is a story of Munoo being knocked from one end to another by his tragic fate like a shuttlecock. The novel is a sad commentary upon the values cherished by the people. Munoo says, "All servants look alike. There must be only two classes of people, the rich and the poor."

Poverty is an evil itself and Munoo is victim of this evil of poverty. He is a miserable creature. He received compassion neither at home nor in society. Anand draws our attention by depicting the scene of Nathu Ram's household where Munoo serves as a servant. It is like a mad house where people seem to be unfamiliar with the feelings of love and compassion. The author shows four stages of Munoo's exploitation from home to society. Anand's reformative role comes to the forefront again when he describes the agony of Munoo as a servant.

Having had a little education, He is more sensitive to the injustice meted out to him by the society. The tyranny of the class-system weighs so much upon his mind that it finally becomes the cause of his death. Bakha's agony is more extrovert whereas Munoo's is from inside. His following extract shows the suppressed desire of Munoo to lead life like his master: Munoo would have liked to shave his beard with a sharp Razor of his master [...] he wanted to become a man.Munoo, when he sees the vast anomaly underlying human behavior says: Why are some men so good and others so bad—some like Prabha and Elephant driver and other like Ganpat and the Policeman who beats me, At the railway station.The excerpt is nothing but a quest of Munoo to find out his place in the vast world and to understand the dichotomy in human behavior that differentiated man. To quote Premila Paul:

> The class system— a permanent theme in literature is in a way inseparable from the caste system so far as the Indian context is concerned since both of them have proved to be exploitative to human dignity.

The impact of class-disparity is more damaging than caste system. To quote Premila Paul again, 'class has certainly proved to be more divisive than caste in Indian society because it is able to affect every section of society at the economic, cultural and political levels.'

It is the first time in Anglo-Indian literature that a writer like Anand tries to lift the image of a boy like Munoo to the level of hero. 'Munoo represents the disinherited and the dispossessed of the earth whose tragic life indicates inhumanity of man to man.' Anand describes in detail Munoo's life thus trying to focus on the sub-standard condition of his life. He finds himself broken in body and spirit. His journey through life—sleeping in city streets, dwelling in slums and living at the edge of starvation—all have been delineated in detail. The severe beatings of his aunt and uncle border on cruelty. His job as a domestic servant is pitiable as he has to clean the vessels, sweep the floor, fetch water and do all kinds of chores and to get abuses in return. He is lost in the cruel world— Prabha's love is a little streak of hope, but in contrast, Ganpat, her husband nullifies all hope by treating him cruelly. Munoo does not understand properly what makes a man superior and is always made conscious that he is inferior. He is again and made to realise his position. Even Prabha's love for him vapors off when there is economic constraint on her. Prabha says, 'I am through with such a scum as you. You are not my class. You belong to the street and there you shall go. I spit on you.' Money decides the identity and status of man. It decides human relationships in our society where virtues of a man remain unrecognized without monetary status. Money can make man a master or servant. Another problem taken up by Anand is that of child-labour. Making children work under abominable conditions for many hours is really very cruel of the society. Thus the novel highlights various malpractices and anomalies going on in Indian society. Anand focuses on these to draw attention so that a better and an egalitarian society may be established where man is not treated on the basis of class and caste.

Two Leaves and a Bud, another novel by Anand depicts the theme of economic exploitation. It elaborately shows the struggle of exiled protagonist against the hostile forces in an alien landscape. This novel draws upon the real life-account of plantation workers in British-owned Tea-Estates in Assam. The British managers used different types of lure to attract them from remote villages of India. Once these laborers arrived in the state, their condition became more or less that of a prisoner left to the mercy of ruthless planters and greedy middlemen. They were constantly ill-treated and put to hard labor. Their women were molested. Any sign of revolt was dealt with a heavy hand. But on the other hand British planters could get away even after committing murders as the judges were white-skinned. Anand's novel is an unvarnished late of the sufferings of peasants in this plutocracy.

Gangu represents this unfortunate community of uprooted peasants trying to negotiate their destiny in the alien landscape of Tea-plantations. Falling prey to the false promises of a cooliecatcher Buta, Gangu allows himself to be transported to the distant unfamiliar Tea-Estate along with his family. He soon finds out that it is a prison without bars, an unbreakable jail. Gangu's life here is one of unrelieved suffering: his wife Sajani dies of malaria; unable to meet the expenses of her funeral he falls into the debt-trap of a moneylender; meanwhile his daughter Leila draws the attention of the roving eyes of the lusty manager Reggie Hunt; and in that followers he is shot dead by the manager. While unfolding Gangu's tale Anand leaves no aspect of plantation life untouched.

Particularly he throws light on the dubious values and dehumanizing motives of British colonizers. The Britishers firmly believed that Indians were too ignorant and barbaric to rule themselves and those they could be controlled only by using force. This force was often shown through the use of baton. These details of maltreatment described in the novel make it a harrowing tale of the life of plantation workers. Poor peasants have been shown engaged in a ceaseless, debased and dehumanizing struggle simply to eke out their lives from day to day.

Anand again highlights the theme of untouchability in The Road published in 1961. He wanted to show that even after independence and political autonomy things have not changed. One-third of Indian citizens, namely Harijans, still remain enslaved in India. Anand felt the need to hammer on the point again as a he himself was a witness to the discrimination and humiliations to which *Harijans* were subjected to in the villages. Bhikhu is the new *avatar* of Bakha. He is literate but the society has not changed and there is no effort to provide dignity to this caste.

His novels seem to convey the message that the poor lot of the bottom dogs is a matter of economic determinism, but it can be reformed by love, compassion, sympathy and a humane consideration of man as man. The suffers are not victims of fate are God only but of society, which is man-made. Social forces play the role of a villain. A committed humanist, he heralds a revolt, a creative struggle to bring about a new society. It is a constructive protest. He recalls:

> I certainly felt, in the midst of my own poetry and exile, the compulsion that it is better not to win applause by conforming to my establishment, to face the privileged order, and to claim the right to notice the existence of men like Bakha.

Anand candidly wrote about the poor with whom he was most familiar. True he immersed himself, "[...] in the sub- world of the poor, the insulted and the injured, through continuous pilgrimages to the villages and small town and big town bastes of our country."

Anand more than any other Indian writer had felt on his pulses the fate of the underdog and the underprivileged that, before him, remained unnoticed in Indian Literature. Anand was much pained to see them crushed under the heavy weight of man-made laws, the scheme of cruelty and exploitation, the decadent and perverted orthodoxy that held Indians in its devilish grip. So intense is the writer's sympathy for the poor and the oppressed that in his novels, we sometimes find the author cry with anguish against injustice, which was so common in those days. In every novel of Anand we see simple noble souls pitted against the soulless poverty of industrialization or labor or priestly exploitation or individual selfishness.

Class distinction and the aristocratic system are repugnant to him because they check the natural and free current of fellow feelings which should flow uninhibited from one man to another. The subjects chosen by Anand are quite reflective of Indian panorama. The only criterion of his choosing a subject is that it should bring to the limelight the miseries and humiliations of the unfortunate victims suffering under different kinds of exploitations. By introducing such an unpleasant subject as cleaning of latrines in his novels, Anand has tried to bring out the hidden practices of the hypocrites. Latrines, dirt, cesspools, poverty, beggary and disease, everything is here beautifully described. By leading caravan of the India of Maharajas and of European officers, but that of real India; of the majority of Indians. His purpose is not so much to draw sentimental tears as to show his readers the true dignity that lies hidden behind the mask of dirt.

Anand ventured into a new territory with his private life of an Indian prince. His choice now fell not on an untouchable or a coolie for his protagonist; instead, he picked up an Indian prince. Victor Edward George Ashok Kumar—the prince of Sham Pur—is a victim of the post-independence policy of Indian government to dissolve the princely states. But he is a bigger victim to the tactics of his selfish, greedy, and ruthless mistress. Anand probes into the political and private life of his protagonist. The emphasis, of course, is on the latter aspect. Anand has projected the putrescence and merger clousness of the glittering and gaudy world of the Indian prince in true colours. Because the protagonist in the novel is no less than a prince who claims, to be demy-god, a descendant of Lord Vishnu via god Rama, no Saviour figure is introduced. The presence of a Saviour is a man of high profile. Anand's artistic sense makes him bring into his novel a reporter instead of a Saviour. This is the only novel in which the protagonist suffers alone; he has nobody to relieve him from the suffering and he himself is not strong enough to stand against his exploitation.

The suffering prince has his retinue—a personal physician, a private secretary an aid de camp, a political secretary, and a number of attendants who are always at his beck and call.

But all of them fail to save their master both from political and personal crises. By virtue of his political authority he stands much above them. All of them are ready to satisfy every whim and caprice of the master to whom they are obliged in one way or another. After the prince's elopement with Bunti Russel, Dr. Shankar observes on the role of the former associates objectively and critically: "I felt like telling munshiji how he had been humbugging himself, talking of Guarding his highness against evil influences when he, captain Partap Singh, the A.D.C. Mr. Bool Chand, the political secretary, and myself indulged every whom and fancy of his Highness, in order to curry favour with him, and shut our eyes to what we did not want to see about his highness, even while we pretended to be so concerned when anything happened. And such indulgence is more expected from the "paid servants" of a prince than their efforts to negate the eccentric ideas of their master. In this master servant relationship, the servants expected their co-operation and help whenever a critical situation arises but they cannot prick the bubble of the kind ego. They can preach sermons, advise him, and apprise him of a situation but they are unable to change his decisions. The absence of the saviour figure, therefore, is according to the demands of the nature of characters.

The absence of the saviour hero is demanded by the period of Indian history in general and the life of victor is particular with which the novel deals. The action of the novel is set in the background of very significant historical events of the merger of princely states into the union of India. All the princes had to sign the instrument of accession. The protests, the persuasions, and the authority of the princes were no avail against the iron will of iron man, Sardar Vallabbhai Patel. Nobody could have saved the prince from such a situation. And the situation worsened particularly with the people of the state turning rebellious. The other aspect of victor problems is his exploitation by his mistress. The aspect is too personal to be dealt with adequately by an outsider. No doubt, the prince discusses many of his troubles with Dr. Hari Shankar, but the latter can at the most warm him against the cunning intrigues of his nymphomaniac mistress. But the maneuvers of Ganga Dasi and the weakness of the schizophrenic victor render his guidance useless. Munshi Mithan Lal religious preaching's too become a subject of ridicule with the prince. Moreover, nobody wants to incur the displeasure till he becomes completely neurotic. Dr. Shankar confesses that "the symptom of his difficulty, of course, was his preoccupation with Gangi. And it had not been possible to remove it, because we had pampered him and made it seem a nice kind of feeling to indulge in under the guise of love, and he had even won sympathy from us in his invalid privileged position." The "privileged position" is, in fact, two fold. He enjoys the privilege of being an authority over his employees and wins their sympathy for being a weakling who has been left mentally invalid by the ruthless behaviour of his selfish and crafty mistress. In both cases the doctor, the secretary and the A.D.C. fail to save him from his predicament.

The immediate impetus behind the writing of the novel too may be one of the reasons of the absence of the saviour character. Anand might have had the idea of writing a novel on an Indian prince beforehand, but the actual impulse was provided by Anand personal rejection by his beloved, a hill woman. The shock led to his neurosis. The novel was written at the advice of his Greek dancer nurse who wanted him to write his agony off. The writing that was a therapy to cure a disease required more the true projection of a situation than aiming at ideological propaganda. He, no doubt, touches upon the theme of the administrative deterioration in the state of sham pur in particular and all princely states in general, but the concentration lies on the personal tragedy of prince victor. Moreover, the princes were already losing their paramountcy; their autocratic administration was giving place to popular governing bodies. At this stage Anand aim of the exposure of their putrescent lives could be a reformative or curative one. The reform had already been introduced by Indian Congress government through curtailment of their powers.

Through the instrument of accusation, "the states acceded to the Dominion of India on the three subjects of defense, external affairs and communication," records V.P. Menon, secretary to Sardar Vallabbhai Patel. Although the "accession did not imply any financial liability on the part of the acceding states," and large privy purses were promised to the princes, the fact remains that these rulers were deprived of much of sovereignty which had been their right for hundreds of years. The corrupting power having been snatched away from the princes, they could no longer trouble their subjects through extortion, exploitation, and injustice.

Anand, therefore, curbs his propagandistic instinct in the novel. He does not require a spokesman to condemn the evil of corrupt administration by the princes. The novel is free from any overt ideological commitment on the part of the novelist. There is no authorial intervention with a purpose to hammer his point home. The novel, therefore, is aesthetically Te best by Anand. The life of the prince is very authentically presented. The characters are delineated without any prejudices for or against them. The convincing and captivating episodes enable a reader to have a clear glimpse of the reality that lies under all the glitter of royal families. Anand contrasts the outer shimmer with the inner sordidness. The contrast becomes all the more glaring when people lose all faith in the autocratic set up; they give up their traditional allegiance to the kind and fight for their rights. "For I realized," remarks Dr. Shankar, "that all this magnificence, the flash and pageantry of the gentry, the polo and the champagne etc, was the decorative outer surface the appearance, of a cryde was reality, underneath which all the decencies of life were symbolically or really crushed and ground in the dust". The decadent life in the royal court of Sham Pur epitomizes the degeneration of moral values in all the states under princely administration. The author prose into the psyche of both the prince and the subjects. With rare insights psyche of both the prince and the subjects. With rare insights rules, he revealed the process of transition of power from majestic administrators to the common people. Though his treatment of the theme is profound that and objectives yet the novel has elicited contradictory critical commentary. Cowasjee finds the novel to be "Anand most impressive work". Jack Lindsay express almost a similar opinion: "we feel the conflict of the old and the new in India with an evocative force that marks this book out as a most impressively sustained marks performance." He goes ahead of Cowasjee to add that "if Anand had written nothing else, his place in the history of the novel would be secure—his place as a profound interpreter of Indian life in a phase of pervasive crisis".

On the contrary Balarama Gupta finds Lindsay comment, "too tall a claim to be valid," for him the novel is a failure, particularly in so far as there is no close integration between his artistic texture and the author's philosophy of humanism." Naik too finds the novel "hardly a profound interpretation of Indian life in a phase of pervasive crisis," It could have been this," remarks Naik, "if it had not been afflicted with the artistic schizophrenia of trying to be at once a case history and a political chronicle." Only a novel with great profoundity defies classification and earns such varying opinions. The fact remains that despite a few limitations the novel is the best by Anand.

Private life of an Indian Prince forms a very authentic portrayal of the schizophrenic prince and his nymphomaniac beloved. It is "a psyche odyssey". Anand reveals deep knowledge of the life of Indian princes and an insight into abnormal psychology. The knowledge at both levels may be traced back to Anand's close study of the life of princes when during World War II he served as a tutor to the prince of Simla. The prince, like the protagonist of his novel, suffered neurosis and had to find haven in a lunatic asylum. To add to the knowledge of abnormal psychology, there are novelist's personal sufferings from a similar mental state. To provide a sufficient commentary on the working of the protagonist psyche, Anand adopts the technique of the introduction of a narrator. Very cleverly he makes the narrator the personal physician of the prince who is privileged to probe into his physical as well as mental ailments. Because victor confides in him the secrets of his personal and political life, the latter becomes a "friend, guide and philosopher" of the former. Because the private life of the prince is inseparably interwoven with his political life, the personal physician is able to scrutinize both the aspects of his life. The first person narration gives to the action more of a semblance of reality. In the author's note on the novel, Anand remarks about the narrator's role:

The neutral 'I' of the first person singular had tended, In this book, to become a character in his own right. Most writers know how a character in a novel sometimes takes control and runs away with the Story. The author had been content to allow Dr. Shankar to take possession of the narrative, as well As become Sancho Panza to the prince's Don. Therefore the 'I' in this novel is not to be mistaken for The author, who has reverted to the Indian tradition of Anonymity and looks on, like Siva's searing third Eye, at the unfolding of this tragic-comedy.

Despite Anand claim of "anonymity," the fact remains that the narrator is Anand himself, the rational part of his split mind whereas victor represents the irrational, abnormal self of Anand during his neurosis. Anand walks on the pages of the novel safely and without any impression of authorial intrusiveness. Dr. Shankar's philosophy is, mutatis, Anand's own as discussed in apology for heroism. Particularly he expresses Anand ideas about religion, philosophy body, soul and life. He articulates Anand's humanism: "I think that in spite of man's bewilderment and confusion about such question as to what he is, how he ought to act and where he is going; he is the final fact of the universe. There is nothing higher and more dignified than human existence". He shares Anand atheism: "I don't believe that there is any power transcending man, who can decide things for him. Man is responsible for gaining or losing his life". It is through the narrator that Anand projects the eccentricity of victor both in his administration and his private life. In fact "there is as much of Anand in his prince as in his narrator, and this partly accounts for the penetrating analysis of the prince's character. Dr. Shankar is the rational side of the author analyzing the irrational side as seen in the prince." The relationship between the prince and Dr. Shankar is comparable to that of the two selves of the split personality of Prufrock in Eliot love song of Alfred J. the rational self and the passionate self. But unlike other spokesmen of Anand in his novels like *Untouchable, Coolies, Two Leaves and a Bud*, and *Gauri*, Dr. Shankar is not a preacher; he is an observer and recorder of the mental state of the prince. He is a physician and consultant to victor, but he is not his saviour. In the novel, the author repeatedly states the actual position of the doctor and tries to make clear that by virtue of his authority the prince advice above his physician. The latter can, at the most, advice him according to the demands of the circumstances, but he cannot be his saviour, the prince, no doubt, confides even the most personal matters in him, but he does not act upon the prescription and advice of the doctor who is a psychoanalyst as well.

Dr. Shankar has jointed service under the prince to work off a scholarship he has availed of for the three years of his medical education abroad. He therefore is bound to stay in debt slavery. The colloquy after the victor bunti escapade makes his position clear: "and knowing as only you do, that his highness is ill and will behave like this again and again, you should, if only because you have learnt to relish the thought of personal freedom and social justice as elementary needs of your mind and body, not be abject like all the other state subjects, but resign before you get involved any further in the tentacles of that courtesy and affection which the maharaja seeks to weave round you, with all his all absorbing ego that knows no bounds. But there is the other voice to remind him of his obligation to the prince and his duty to his profession:

> "if you owe the money and cannot pay it off immediately and have owe the position you are in, it is not easy to get out of it, especially because you still believe that you may be able to help maharaja to get well and divert him from the path on which he is traveling".

At any rate, it is your duty as a doctor to enable him to regain his confidence in himself, which has been shattered by Ganga Dasi, and to see him adjust himself to some kind of balanced social behavior, but the impact of Ganga's sex tactics is so deep that it renders the prince incorrigible. His sovereignty, moreover, makes him immune to any reformative attempts by any member of his retinue. Dr. Shankar although he enjoys a privileged position among the other employees of victor, again and again feels that he is "the willing slave", the courtier who is cowed down by the refulgent aura of his highness prestige, which was always an omnipresent to reality to us all. Because of the consciousness of victor authority, Dr. Shankar fails to saves him from the maddening intrigues of Ganga Dasi and the crafty plans of his political adversaries. He keeps pondering over the relationship of victor with his mistress and his political reveals but the facts become only "rare and precious pieces of information, curious in the museum of knowledge about human affairs that I was building up, to put in medical terms, an important case history for my files", confess Dr. Hari. This case history becomes attractive materials for narration as Dr. Shankar feels that "to expunge the dread, perhaps it would be a good idea to recapitulate and write down my experiences of victor, for in that way I could attempt a conscious appreciation of my erroneous life. I could find confirmation of my new belief from my memories, the conviction of the preciousness of my integrity that I had let slip through the compromises of the last few years". He also realizes that by losing his integrity, he had not been able to save his master and patient from ultimate neurosis. Instead while "in the pay of the Maharaja", The (the) narrator in this way is only an observer and recorder of the working of victor mind; he is not able to save the prince from the grim situation of his life. The relief that the prince gets from his company is that of giving an outlet to his emotions through a discussion of even the most personal aspects of his life. It is only when victor is flung into the lunatic asylum of Pune that he feels free and thinks of leading an intrinsic life. After Dr. Shankar responsibility is transferred to Dr. Bhagwat of the lunatic asylum, the farmer's reaction is not that of sorrow or regret over the fate of the prince; it is a feeling of relief and freedom from a burden. Now he wants to work for the poor people. He realizes that he has been a coward, a weak willed character who could not resist the sham pur. He never feels committed to save his patient from his predicament. He can only make the latter aware of certain facts of life. His feelings observations, statements, and reaction do provide wholeness to the action of the novel; his commentary provides a touch of authenticity to the portrayal of prince life; but his presence does not save the protagonist from mental derangement.

The other members of the prince's retinue, his political secretary, Munshi Lal and his A.D.C. captain Partap Singh also fail to save their prince. They, instead, worsen the situation by pandering to every whim and fancy of the prince. Munshi Lal, the pedagogic, parsimonious, religious boor—has to stay in the thankless job for money which he requires for the education of his three sons. He is an expert statesman but he becomes a butt of victor jokes. He has picked up some knowledge about the philosophy of celebrities like Emerson, Gandhi and Bhagwan Krishna. Having committed to memory some of the quotation from scriptures he tries to sober the prince by quoting them according to the demands of the occasion. But he is not able to change, the prince's mind which, we are told, was "set on other, more pleasant, things than whole men and their wise maxims". When Ganga Dasi elopes with Bool Chand and the prince is undergoing a spell of profound depression, he comes out with a hackneyed counsel: "then you must forget her and face your loneliness. Once you face the fact that each man is ultimately alone, you will be able to conquer your lower nature and be free". He warns victor against carnal passions: the entrails are the seat of the carnal, animal, lower self, the Kama loka! This carnal ego grows like a cancer at the very roots of life and eats away the soul, destroying the exalted harmony of life, and it causes violent conflicts in the self, which drown all calm and peace with their shrieking and noise". But this Vedanta's philosophy loses its appeal before the suggestion of Partap Singh: "leave the sermons of main mithu alone, we will go to the Hawa palace and have some fun". Having another woman to fill the gap of Ganga Dasi is a welcome suggestion to get out of the traumatic situation. The impact of the murder makes victor completely neurotic. He, in this way, is too weak to protest against any desire of the prince.

This gratification of every caprice of the prince, instead of relieving him, enmeshes him more and more in sensual life. Captain Partap Singh, with his more own lustful and base desires, is always at the disposal of the prince to arrange girls for him whenever the latter is in a mood of dejection because of the ruthless behavior of Ganga Dasi. Anand portrays a very ugly picture of the A.D.C. uncouth lusty a good boozer, a voracious eater and with nothing in his head, except a little white matter under the bun of his long hair. But the uncouth manners are mitigated by his hearty laugh, his generosity and the prodigal warmth of his uncivilized nature.

The touch physique of Partap Singh comes to the rescue of the prince when he is washerman of Annandale because of his adulterous relations with the letters wife. But he feels that he cannot save victor from the hands of Mr. Russel after his escapade with the later daughter. Captain Partap Singh feels the pulse of victor better than Dr. Shankar. When the doctor and the Munshi Lal over victor situation after Ganga Dasi elopement with the political secretary, the captain feel that the solution to victor despondency is that some other girl should be brought to replace Ganga Dasi. While in England, he suggests that June withers can be suitable for the pleasures of victor. He helps victor in arranging a meeting with the girl and winning her over. The colludes with the prince in having Bool Chand murdered. The prince confides in him all the secrets of the plot of murder whereas even Dr. Shankar is kept out of the planning. But Captain Partap Singh, instead of saving victor from the traumatic situation, helps in hastening his lunacy. Victor indulgence in sexual pleasures which the captain arranges cannot make him forget Ganga Dasi. The feeling of dejection becomes rather keener because of the contrast of other girl with Ganga. The murder of Bool Chand leaves victor completely of the prince, he tries to cater to the sensual needs of victor; but he is not able to nor does he try to, save victor from disintegration. Because no saviour characters are introduced and there is no attempt at propaganda, nothing impedes an objective portrayal of the chief characters—victor and Ganga Dasi. Although the life of the prince is dismal and that of Ganga Dasi abominable, it is not exaggerated or diminished with a purpose. The history of princely India abounds in examples of the princes who led even more perverted lives. The portrayal of Victor and Ganga is a fine example of Anand's deep knowledge of the material of the novel and profound observation of the working of human psyche. He studies the problems of Prince Ashok Kumar from two aspects— sociological and psychological. The two aspects are so intricately interwoven that they appear to be almost indistinguishable. The one becomes one of the causes behind the other. Sociologically, victor has inherited absolute sovereignty over his subjects. But power, as usual, has corrupted him socially and personality.

Summing, up the social life of victor, Balarama Gupta aptly remarks that he is "an eccentric Indian prince... Wallowing in sloth and sex, squandering the state money, sucking the life blood of his subjects by inflicting varieties of illegal taxes on them, and stubbornly refusing to merge his state into Indian union after independence. He has had his childhood spent in his father's Zenana and has learnt filthy manners from the court servants. During his boyhood, he has had all his wayward fancies fulfilled. His faulty education at queen marries school. He has snapped all relations with his first two wives; he neglects the third for pleasing his mistress Ganga Dasi. His moral degradation is suitably matched by his mistress's crafty manners. The problems in victor's administration of his state start because of his irresistible passion for Ganga Dasi. She has the son of the Tikyali Rani murdered so that her own son should be declared an heir to the prince. Prince Ashok, blindly devoted to the cunning mistress as he is, fails to see through the greed selfishness, and cruelty of this seductive woman. The coquettish approach of Ganga Dasi persuades woman. The coquettish prince to hold a darbar and declare her son the successor to the throne. To start trouble for the prince, the government refuses to accept the illegitimate son as an heir. She starts her campaign against the decision by contacting the political department of the government. Already the government is displeased with the maladministration in the state and the grievances of people against exorbitant taxes and extortions, the practices which again, are resorted to satisfy the fabulous demands of the greedy mistress who "was the real power behind the throne".

The government, therefore, conducts an enquiry into the matter of the acknowledgment of the illegitimate child as successor. People too start a movement against the unfair administration and form a Praja Mandal which is supported by the Indian national congress. During the enquiry, the allegations of illegal exactions, deprivations, and oppression are well substantiated. The government, therefore, imposes certain restraints on the powers and his authority; he is also plundered of much property by his scheming mistress. To please her, victor tries to gratify all her demands and disposes of not only much of his personal property and jewelry, but also a large part of the state property. He, in this way, is impoverished in two ways—in money and in authority.

The prince is a weakling, a schizohrene who, despite his awareness of the right and the wrong, is not morally strong enough to stand for the right. Physical pleasures so absorb his body and soul that he forgets his administrative duties and responsibilities completely. He knows about the ignoble past of Ganga Dasi; he knows about her present illegitimate relations with many men; he personally observes her in embrace with Dewan Raghbir Singh and in bed with Kurt Landauer during the hunt; but they cannot give her up.

"She is a bitch, but I can't do without her!" confesses victor to Dr. Hari Shankar. That Ganga Dasi possesses him completely is well revealed in the prince helpless conditions: "the bitch she comes to me with so many love words, shrieks and hisses that I—well, I like to sleep with her, you see! And she has got me… I am trapped, I tell you, and I am like a rat in a hole..." Dr Shankar warning—"she will destroy you emotionally, physically, spiritually. She is an untamed jungle. And she will suck your life blood and then spit you out. Get rid of her! She is a completely unscrupulous woman"—falls flat on his ears. The seductive power of the harlot is more powerful than the warning by his friends. Even when Ganga Dasi has jilted him to elope with Bool Chand, victor is not as full of anger against her as he is of desire for reunion with her. He pines for her like as he is of desire for reunion with her. He pines for her like a love-lorn romantic: "if only she would come back, I would take her to some enchanted land, to Kashmir, to Southern France, and I would lead her to the sea, or to some rock, where no one could see us, and where everything would be enchanted as in a fairyland, and there I would have her under a blue sky". His regret is not that he ever loves such a fickle minded and selfish woman; she instead, repents: "oh why was I so thoughtless? Why didn't I give her all that she wanted—houses and land and money and jewellery? The idea of renouncing the world and going to Benaras is only a fleeting one. And even this idea is combined with the desire that Gangi should be with him and they should be dedicated to god.

Such is the spell of sexual pleasures which Ganga Dasi provides that victor is completely oblivious of his administrative responsibilities. He does not realize that people are rising in a "bloodless revolution" against him. Intoxicated by the feeling of inherited kingship, he goes on believing that his people are enjoying the comforts of *Ram Raj*. He ignorantly feels that he is an ideal ruler: "I too want a state in which the raja and Praja can live as father and sons. I want to renew in the people the belief that I have their interests at heart... I am not like the other rulers who despite their people!" The irony is that he never thinks of the interests of his people. As a consequence of undue suppression, people have turned revolutionary. The revolutionary spirit is obvious in the reaction of Buta, the professional hunter, to the prince's Rebuke, in the letter of the detents to Dr. Hari Shankar, in the slogan rising against firing by the prince at the rally of the people shouting alogans. The imagery adumbrates the downfall of the prince which is in the offing: "the sun had gone down and the sky was luminous as though we were going towards the regions of hell, where the blood of victims in the temple of Kali on Siva's hill, and their shrieks, were shooting up to the heavens, for the pink and orange steaks of pain limned the horizon. The sky at the time of sunset, which otherwise presents a feast to the aesthetic eye, seems pain marred. That the mahraja has been deprived of much of his authority is obvious from the fact that when he starts from shimla after his escapade with Bunti Russel, the salute of thirteen guns is reduced to one of seven and at this arrival at sham pur; no Guns are fired at all. The reduction is salutation is a great humiliation for the prince. But the greater humiliations at the hands of Ganga Dasi make him great the shrinking of his political esteem and authority. The actual realization of his political esteem and authority. The actual realization of his downfall comes when he has to sign the instrument of accession under the commanding and rigid behaviour of Sardar Patel. After he has come back as a defeated, dethroned monarch, the disinherited of his mistress too. His shock is much greater at the loss of Ganga Dasi to his political rival, bool Chand, than the loss of his sovereignty. He is on the verge of madness. The madness however, is postponed a little by his instant pleasure with June withers in England. But intense jealousy is not to be suppressed by these momentary pleasures. And he does nothing less than murder Bool Chand, the new paramour of his mistress. The moral and legal repercussions of the crime are sufficient to complete the neurosis to which he has been moving by slow degrees.

Anand's hero, in this way, is a weak kneed, gutless character. He lacks the confidence, courage boldness, and initiative of Manohar protagonist, prince Hiroji of Begward. No doubt, the two princes suffer many similar political and personal troubles, but unlike his counterpart in Anand novel prince has a power of quick decisions and sticks to them. He reveals wonderful fearlessness when he meets his death after he has signed the instrument of accession, rather the "instrument of destruction," as the narrator in the princes calls it. Milk (Mulk) Raj Anand attributes his protagonist's weak will to the circumstances under which he has been brought up. Anand, like a psychiartrist (psychiatrist), probes into the mental upbringing of his hero. Prince ashok Kumar, according the novelist, is a hopelessly ill-adjusted personality because in him there is a confused amalgamation of two civilizations—the values of the feudal order he has inherited and those of the new era in which he is living. Anand presents the clash between these two divergent forces: "the spirits of his dead ancestors were pulling him towards the old virtues, prowess, splendour, firmness, dexterity, generosity, heroism in battle and the other duties of the high-caste superior, kshatriya, prince, while a number of new demons, the fashions of the hour, were pulling him into another direction". The conflict resulted in the irrational, indecisive, weak, and cowardly behaviours of the prince. Anand's introduction of the prince prepares the readers for the final fate that he meets. Anand observes "all his scandalous behaviours, therefore, was due to the incongruity of the various strains in him that were trying to unite and become one person, but only made him a kind of montage man, a pathetic creature, a spoilt child". And the behaviour of victor throughout the novel bears out the introductory sketch of his personality. Still the novel does not give any impression of having been written according to a preconceived plan. That it is a spontaneous expression becomes clears from the fact that the novel "rushed out of me in one month" at a suggestion by his nurse.

Anand concentrates on the highly irrational, whimsical, and ignoble behaviour of Prince Ashok Kumar, but the character of the prince as drawn by Anand does not offend credibility. The presentation of the life of the maharaja is rather a fine example of restraint on material by the author if we keep in mind the reckless orgies, merry-making, drinking, hunting, womanizing, and feasting in the courts of real Indian princes. For example, it is said that the harem of the Maharaja of Patiala (Patiala), consisted of three hundred and fifty women and he had a new religion started for the fifty women and he had a new religion started for the appeasement of sex-urge. His "*palace of Gaiety*" was unmatched for the atmosphere of merry-making. Again, the eccentricity of victor is much less in comparison with that of the prince of Junagarh who celebrated the marriage of his bitch roshnara of the dog bobby of the nawab with rare pomp and show. On the occasion, "the state holiday was declared for three days and all citizens and guests at their residence by special wagons and trucks, three times a day, morning, afternoon and evening, while the rulers and the distinguished guests were entertained more lavishly with sumptuous good and songs by beautiful dancing girls from Baroda, Bombay and Indore." The narration of the ceremony by Diwan Germany Das is, in fact, a commentary on the impetuosity of the prince. The behaviour of victor in the administrative sphere, particularly at the singing the instrument of accession again, is without exaggeration by the novelist. Most of the princes ignored state affairs for they were too busy merry-making. Regarding the signing of the instrument all princes, were naturally, reluctant as it meant giving up authority notwithstanding the promises by the government that they would go on enjoying authority and liberty. Maharaja Hanwant Singh of Jodhpur who was persuaded with much difficulty to sign the instrument whipped out a revolver and threatening V. P. Menon, the chief secretary of Sardar Patel, Said: "I refuse to accept your dictation." It was only because of the appropriate of Lord Mountbatten at that time that the attempt to kill Mr. Menon was foiled. All these instances from history reveal that Anand has shown great restraint. He has not tried to tilt the scales against the eccentric prince. The portrayal is remarkable for the authenticity which has been a result of the novelist's deep knowledge of psycho—analysis. He analyses the condition of the prince not merely as a doctor, but also with great sympathy as a fellow human being. That is why we find that "despite the prince's moral and political corruption the novel's major emphasis is not in the tyrannical abominations of a Marxian ogre but the in pathetic anguish of a fallen autocrat. The fictional presentation of historical materials through psychological treatment makes the novel a grand success.

Anand is more severe in his treatment of his heroine Ganga Dasi —a nymphomaniac a "consummate concubine," a non professional harlot, a human vampire, and a viper of a woman. Both Anand and his critics are lavish in showering negative epithets on the woman whose intrigues are a cause of victor's downfall. But the severity of Anand does not make him waver from the path of authenticity and truthfulness. He not only presents her as "absolute promiscuity" but also traces her past to relate the psyche of the nymphomaniac to the circumstances in which she had her birth and upbringing.

Ganga Dasi has had a past full of variegated sexual experiences. Her past has subjected her to a variety of emotions aroused by her relations with a large number of lovers. Having had an unhappy married life with a Brahmin peon, a drunkard to whom she was sold, she developed attraction for other men. Already being the daughter of a harlot, she had acquired the manners of a woman of pleasure. And before she was fourteen, she had been taken by many herdsmen of the village. After marriage too she changed one lover for another without any hesitation. She is a veritable nymphomaniac accepting without resistance the advances of any man who comes to her though she cannot stick to anybody. The pitfall in the psychology of a nymphomaniac is that she will believe that her next victim will be last," says Dr. Shankar, "whereas there is an infinite regress in this business". Her behaviour has its explanation in the peculiar relationship between her father and mother. Her father was a priest and brought fruit and clothes to Gangi. The daughter, therefore, loves the father. But the father suspected Gangi's mother and often beat her ruthlessly. Gangi (Ganga) therefore loathed the tyrant in him. Now in every man she finds her father figure. She is fascinated towards the hero but abhors the tyrants. Her experiences have left her "just a bundle of ill-assorted nerves, impulses and fancies bound up into a knot, as is the peasant woman's bundle, the knot being symbolic of the sharp, instinctive sense of mastery she had of all situations". Victor found in her an appropriate companion because he too was promiscuous and his wife, Indira was too polished and cultured for his crude manners: I had behaved badly to my wives, and she had been bad. So I thought that two bad people might make a good pair.

But Ganga Dasi proves to be much worse than the childish simple, weak-willed, and impetuous victor. She is a "consummate actress" whose tactics of sex inveigle the prince so strongly that he feels that "she is bound up with my entrails". He knows about her past love affairs but is inescapably caught in her grip. Such is his fascination for her that he accepts her everytime (every time) she has been in bed with somebody else. Her green eyes entice all men, particularly victor, so strongly that they become blind to the fact that she is using her arts of love-making to rob them of their wealth. She attracts a man with her love-words and well trained sex practices pretending to be a child wanting protection, but once she gets the victim in her grip, she possesses him body and soul. The brief moments of pleasure that victor has enjoyed in bed with her are sufficient to make her seem indistinguishable from his life. When victor comes into contact with her, he is so pleased with her love-making that he feels "that someone had come into my life, someone who knows the life of a town life Lahore amidst all these yokels, someone to cling to in the midst of all the artificiality of the state where I was a kind of tin god. To have a private life with someone devoted to you after all the ballyhoo of pomp and splendour! And she was a lovely companion and gave me such assurance. I could work ten times harder because I had a satisfactory personal life". But all this assurance and devotion were amrerepretence to snatch away the money, property, and jewellery from the prince. Once she has entered into the life of victor, she dominates him so completely that there cannot be a place for any other woman in his life. She has victor's wife Indira confined to a lonely place; she has Indira's son murdered so that she may have her own son declared a *Tikka*. And victor is under such a spell of her charm that he concedes her wishes and acknowledges her son is his own or is fathered by the Raja Sahib of Badaun with whom she has had an affair before coming into his own life. Such is the hold of Gangi on victor that when he goes to see indira and is moved by a feeling of affection for her son, he is "embarrassed that some servant might see him in this tender relation with his child by Indira and report to Gangi". And when Gangi comes to know about the visit to his wife, she turns victors out of her room at night. She has such a possessive and egoistic nature hat "always she strained to be the centre of attraction, the sun towards which all the sunflowers must turn". It is partly to satisfy her enormous ego that she takes one lover after another.

Ganga Dasi wants victor, like her other lovers, to cling to her but she herself cannot cling to anybody. She wants all attention from her lover, but herself she is thinking of her other lovers even while making love. She can discard her lover us soon as she finds that he can no longer gratify her greed for wealth. She makes victor extort money from poor peasants and bestow it on her. She makes him sell public property for the satisfaction of her insatiable desires. But as soon as she finds that he is disinherited of his authority, her green eyes turn to victor's rival himself because she hopes that Bool Chand will enjoy a good status in the popular government. With her meanness and selfishness, she stands as a foil Tikyali Rani who though jilted by victor for his preference for Gangi, comes to serve her husband in the lunatic asylum. Anand appropriately describes her as a "schizoid" a split personality at once sadist and masochist. Anand like a psychiatrist trying to diagnose the mental ailment of a patient scrutinizes the problems of a Ganga Dasi. He however deduces that, "since everyman had been a kind of cruel father to her, she loves and hated men in an ambivalence which resulted in the woman's Amazonian revenge against man."

Anand's attempt to psycho-analyse the behavior of Ganga Dasi has a humanistic element in it. He not only gives a statement about her character or merely presents her as a hateful, immoral concubine but is fair enough to cast the blame on the circumstances that have moulded her personality. He tries to prove into the basic cause which can dehumanize a person. Although Ganga Dasi appear more abominable than Victor, Anand is no less fair to his heroine than to his hero. If Gangi (Ganga) is worse in her behavior, it is so,

Anand reveals, because she has suffered more. The fact that the novel deals with both the public and private life of the pricne (prince) needs the emphasis to be more on the actions of victor than those of Ganga Dasi who enjoys no public status. Dr. Paul other charge that the reader has very little direct contact with her and that her character is more often described than depicted too has a clear explanation. It is that Ganga Dasi is not a public figure. Her status is that she is a keep, a mistress — a lady whose chief function is to provide pleasure to her lover in very moment. Such a woman cannot be expected to act much publicly. All that this hypnotic but illiterate woman is fit for is to use her sexual attractiveness for acquiring wealth. That too requires more of insidious plans than clearly avowed aims.

Anand, is this way, has been as successful in handling the victims of psychic problems as he has been of treating the victims of social and economic problems. To deprecate the novel merely as a clinical study would be unfair because the novelist has presented a beautiful blend of history, psychology, and fiction. Moreover, his choice of a psychological problem as a subject of his novel is well in keeping with the modern trend in literature. The novel, in fact, is a bigger artistic success than his untouchable or coolie because here there is no saviour character to hold the stage for a long time and impede the progress of the story through long, propagandistic speech. The narrator no doubt, at certain places voices Anand philosophy, but the speeches are well embedded in the dialogues. The narrator himself is weak willed and timid like the prince and though a good friends, is not a saviour character. Through skillfully handled episodes, the novelist presents the journey of his protagonist from eccentricity to lunacy. Without exaggeration he presents the failure of his hero in both public and private life. The relationship between the hero and the heroine eludes scrutiny and description— the fact in which lies the greatness of literary art of the novelist.

Bibliography

Anand, M.R. *Untouchable*. London: Lawrence & Wishart, 1935.

Anand, M.R. *Coolie.* London: Lawrence & Wishart, 1936.

Anand, M.R. *Two leaves a bud*. London: Lawrence & Wishart, 1937.

Anand, M.R. *Private Life of an Indian Prince*. London: Hutchinson international, 1953.

Anand, M.R. *Preface to Two Leaves and a Bud*. Bombay: Kutub Popular, 1951.

Anand, M.R. *Untouchable*. Bombay: Kutub Popular, 1935.

Anand, M.R. *Untouchable*. Penguine Books India, 1993.

Anand, M.R. *Little Plays of Mahatma Gandhi*. New Delhi: Arnold Publications, 1991.

Bhatnagar M.K. *The Insights into the Novels of R.K. Narayan*. New Delhi: Atlantic Publishers, 2002.

Bhattacharya, B. *So Many Hungers*. Delhi: Orient Paperbacks, 1978.

C. J. George, Mulk Raj Anand, His Art and Concerns: A Study of

His Non-autobiographical Novels, New Delhi: Atlantic Publishers, 1994.

Chand, T. *History of the Freedom Movement in India*. New Delhi: Govt. of India Publications, 1992.

Cowasjee, Saros. So Many Freedoms: A Study of the Major Fiction of Mulk Raj Anand, New Delhi: Oxford University Press, 1977.

Dhawan, R.K., ed. *The Novels of Mulk Raj Anand*. New York: Prestige, 1992.

Forster, E.M. *Preface to Untouchable*. London: Lawrence & Wishart, 1935.

Nagarajan, K. *Chronicles of Kedaran*. Bombay: Asia Publications, 1961.

Naik, M.K. *A History of Indian English Literature*. New Delhi: Sahitya Academy, 1982.

Nayak, H.M. *Welcome Speech in National Seminar on Gandhiji in Indian Literature, Mysore, 1970*. Karnataka: University of Karnataka Press, 1971.

Narayan, R.K. *The Vendor of Sweets*. Mysore: Indian Thought Publications, 1967.

Paul, Premila. *The Novels of Mulk Raj Anand: A Thematic Study*. New Delhi: Sterling Publishers, 1983.

Rao, R. *Kanthapura*, Madras: Oxford University Press, 1938.

Shailaja B. Wadikar, "Silent Suffering and Agony in Mulk Raj Anand's Untouchable", in Amar Nath Prasad and Rajiv K. Malik, Indian English Poetry and Fiction: Critical Elucidations, Volume 1, New Delhi: Sarup & Sons, 2007, p. 144–155.

Sitaramaiah, P. *Gandhi In His Many Aspects*. Bombay: Jaico, 1986.

Index

• • •